Contributions to Economics

More information about this series at http://www.springer.com/series/1262

Elena G. Popkova • Yakov A. Sukhodolov

Foreign Trade as a Factor of Economic Growth

Russian-Chinese Foreign Trade Cooperation

Elena G. Popkova
Volgograd State Technical University
Volgograd, Russia

Yakov A. Sukhodolov
Baikal State University
Irkutsk, Russia

ISSN 1431-1933　　　　　　　ISSN 2197-7178　(electronic)
Contributions to Economics
ISBN 978-3-319-45984-4　　　ISBN 978-3-319-45985-1　(eBook)
DOI 10.1007/978-3-319-45985-1

Library of Congress Control Number: 2016952240

© Springer International Publishing AG 2017
This work is subject to copyright. All rights are reserved by the Publisher, whether the whole or part of the material is concerned, specifically the rights of translation, reprinting, reuse of illustrations, recitation, broadcasting, reproduction on microfilms or in any other physical way, and transmission or information storage and retrieval, electronic adaptation, computer software, or by similar or dissimilar methodology now known or hereafter developed.
The use of general descriptive names, registered names, trademarks, service marks, etc. in this publication does not imply, even in the absence of a specific statement, that such names are exempt from the relevant protective laws and regulations and therefore free for general use.
The publisher, the authors and the editors are safe to assume that the advice and information in this book are believed to be true and accurate at the date of publication. Neither the publisher nor the authors or the editors give a warranty, express or implied, with respect to the material contained herein or for any errors or omissions that may have been made.

Printed on acid-free paper

This Springer imprint is published by Springer Nature
The registered company is Springer International Publishing AG
The registered company address is: Gewerbestrasse 11, 6330 Cham, Switzerland

Foreword

When globalization takes place, there is a complex transformation of the world's economic system and the foreign economic relations of its participants. The influence of globalization on economic processes is ambiguous and is treated differently by different scholars. On the one hand, globalization stimulates the development of international trade and transnational entrepreneurship, stimulates global competition and innovations, and stimulates the rationalization of the economy on a global scale, because it ensures the free movement of resources and products through a highly effective market mechanism.

On the other hand, not all participants in international economic relations gain profit from them. It provides the largest advantages to countries that manage the process and possess the necessary preconditions for transnationalization of their economies and businesses. Countries that were the last to open up their economies and join the process of globalization are the sources of development for leading countries, and occupy a peripheral position in the global economy. As a result, the differentiation between countries in the global economic system grows over time.

This book studies the possibilities provided by globalization for all countries regardless of their level of socio-economic development and the length of time they have had an open economy. It provides a possible solution to the problems of economic globalization through elimination of its negative consequences and maximization of its advantages, as related to activating economic growth in underdeveloped countries.

Historical and economic preconditions and problems of modern foreign trade cooperation between Russia and China are reflected in multiple works by contemporary Russian scholars and Chinese economists who study the issues related to strengthening of the role of China in the global economy, cooperation of Russia and China in the sphere of foreign trade, and expansion of economic cooperation and development of bilateral relationship.

However, despite the range of works that have characterized various aspects of foreign trade cooperation between Russia and China, issues surrounding further development of foreign trade in individual regions and in the country as a whole have not been studied completely. The works of contemporary economists do not pay enough attention to solutions for the problems and contradictions of modern foreign trade relations between Russia and China.

Study of the formation of completely new directions for Russian–Chinese foreign trade cooperation in order to modernize the Russian economy and develop it more dynamically in view of the resource potential of specific regions is of particular interest. Chinese experience in the organization of foreign trade cooperation should be studied in more detail. These circumstances have predetermined the choice of research topic.

This research consists of the expansion of theoretical ideas about foreign trade as a factor of influence on the development of Russia's national economy and the vector of its economic growth under the conditions of globalization, and development of recommendations for improving foreign trade cooperation with its strategic partner—China—in order to modernize the national economy. The following subjects are explored:

Study of the conceptual foundations of economic growth under the conditions of globalization;
Conduct of problem analysis of "underdevelopment whirlpools" as an obstacle for economic growth;
Consideration of theoretical aspects and evolution of the establishment of international trade;
Defining the role of foreign trade for development of the national economy under modern conditions;
Evaluation of the Russian economy's readiness for development of foreign trade cooperation;
Substantiation of the necessity for developing cooperation between Russia and China in the sphere of foreign trade;
Determination of the main directions of modernization for the Russian economy in view of the "Asian" factor in the development of the country's foreign trade connections;
Development of state regulation and support for the development of Russia's economic interests as regards foreign trade cooperation with China.

The book contains fundamental conclusions, practical examples, and recommendations. The research will be interesting for theoretical scholars and practitioners who deal with economic growth, foreign economic cooperation, and economic globalization. The study has not only theoretical but also educational value, and suggests to readers further research in this sphere. Readers will learn much about the sense and role of foreign trade cooperation so that economic growth can take place under the conditions of globalization, and will also be able to come to their own conclusions about this issue.

Volgograd State University Alla E. Kalinina
Volgograd, Russia

Contents

1 Introduction 1
2 Theoretical Aspects of Economic Growth in the Globalizing World ... 5
   2.1 Conceptual Foundations of Economic Growth in the
       Globalizing World 5
   2.2 Problem Analysis of "Underdevelopment Whirlpools"
       as Obstacles for Economic Growth 17
3 Foreign Trade as a Vector of Economic Growth in the Globalizing
   World 25
   3.1 Foreign Trade: Theoretical Aspects and Evolution
       of Establishment 25
   3.2 Role of Foreign Trade in the Development of National
       Economies in the Modern World 34
4 Role and Meaning of Foreign Trade Cooperation in the Globalizing
   World Through the Example of Russia and China 47
   4.1 Evaluation of Readiness of Russia's Economy for Development
       of Foreign Trade Cooperation 47
   4.2 Substantiation of the Necessity for Development of Cooperation
       Between Russia and China in Foreign Trade 63
5 Perspectives of Acceleration of the Rates of Economic Growth
   of Russia in the Context of Foreign Trade Cooperation with China ... 75
   5.1 Main Directions of the Modernization of the Russian Economy
       in View of the "Asian" Factor of the Country's Developing
       Foreign Trade Connections 75
   5.2 Measures of State Regulation and Cooperation for the
       Realization of Russia's Economic Interests in Foreign
       Trade Cooperation with China 93

5.3 Directions of Change of Raw Materials Vector of the Development of the Economy of the Siberian Federal District and Irkutsk Oblast in Relation to the Development of Foreign Trade Relations between Russia and China.................................... 102

Conclusions.. 115

References... 123

Chapter 1
Introduction

Economic growth and the mechanisms of its management are among the most important problems of economic theory. The significance and importance of these issues in modern economic research is confirmed by the high frequency with which the Nobel Prize is awarded to those researchers who study particular aspects of them. Among the most significant works are those by Kuznets (1971), Schultz and Lewis (1979), Solow (1987) and other Nobel Prize winners. In Russian economic tradition, the study of the problems of economic growth was largely influenced by Marxist theory, with its ideas about the evolution of means of production and forms of economic relations in society. In economic science in Russia today, there is also a special role for institutional economy, and many original concepts and theoretical approaches to the study of economic growth are offered within this context.

Related to this, it is necessary to note the failure to explore the problems of theoretical character and fundamental research in the economy. Theories do not take into account the fact that applied developments are subject to commercialization, which—because specialist scientific schools are poorly financed—is a decisive factor in choosing the direction of scientific activity. An area of fundamental research in this area, which requires additional attention, is the development of approaches to studying the quality of economic growth in Russian regions.

The new quality of economic growth that is described in this book is studied through the universalization of ideas about the nature of macro-economic dynamics, seeing this as a succession of qualitative transfers from certain states to other states as the means of production changes. Let us view the main provisions of this concept and their meaning in the development of a strategy for the long-term development of Russia's economy in the modern world.

Fundamental to the new quality of economic growth that is observed in this book is the concept of qualitative transition from the old to the new method of public production. According to this, economic growth can be viewed as a process and the result of the performance of various types of qualitative transitions: material, demographic, institutional, and globalizing. Thus, the new quality of economic growth appears while the means of public production are transformed, as a result of definable qualitative transitions. The transition from old to new takes place as the means of public production changes, and expresses the general tendency of the economy to develop progressively. This framework allows us to understand the sense in which the global economic system is transformed through the establishment of dialectic connection between its old and new states, thereby allowing for evaluation of the transitional processes which take place as new means of production gradually replace the old ones.

In different countries—depending on the level of socio-economic development that has been achieved and the level of interaction with the external world—various types of qualitative transitions are realized simultaneously. In the most developed states, material, demographic, and institutional transitions have been completed, and a globalizing transition is underway.

In the Russian economy, only material and demographic transformations are taking place, while development of an institutional environment in the economy is still at a low level, and the character of interaction with the external environment is not changing fast. Thus, it is possible to state that "in the globalizing world, Russia requires not only economic growth in its qualitative expression, but change of its quality, manifesting in innovational character of development, capable of providing the competitiveness of Russian manufacturers both in the internal and global markets".[1]

Unfortunately, the regions of Russia fall behind in terms of economic development when compared with the developed countries and regions of the world. Moreover, the speed at which this is being reversed is not optimal. According to rough estimates, Russia will need 20–40 years to approach the USA's level of development with regard to the GDP (gross domestic product) per capita indicator.

Based on the materials used in this book, it is possible to draw conclusions about the expediency of implementing the theoretical and practical aspects of research into the new quality of economic growth, as part of strategic planning at national and regional levels. Expanding planning and applying theoretical analysis will allow us to form new and effective approaches to the development of Russia's economy.

Taking into account the conditions in which the global economy is developing, it appears from forecasts that Russia can play a special role as it begins to search for directions in which it can modernize and tools which it can use in order to transition to an innovative path. This is important so that the country can overcome its lack of achievement, when compared with the leading countries of the world, and modernize its economy, providing dynamic and sustainable economic growth.

A significant move in this direction could be made by changing the way in which foreign trade activities are organized, diversifying the commodities that are exported so that more of them have a high level of processing or added value.

---

[1]Shakhovskaya, L.S. New Prospects of Economic Growth: Modern Vision Paradigm/L.S. Shakhovskaya, E.G. Popkova//Global Business and Economics Anthology.—2006.—Vol. I, December.—P. 428–439.—Eng.

This will allow Russia to strengthen and expand the most valuable segments in the global commodity markets that it currently holds, leaving behind the orientation of exports towards raw materials of export, thereby modernizing the economy and increasing national competitiveness.

It is very difficult for Russia to achieve these aims utilizing only its own forces, as it has socio-economic and foreign policy limitations. Russia needs a reliable, powerful, and interested partner, motivated for long-term cooperation. The dynamic development of Asian countries—especially China—in the twenty-first century and successful Russian–Chinese cooperation, and existing political, trade, and economic agreements between the two countries, open new perspectives for changing trade cooperation. The leading role in this process may belong to the regions of Russia that have large potential for development and in which China is a leading foreign trade partner.

Therefore, the change in foreign trade cooperation between Russia and China in the context of a quickly growing Asian vector in the global economy, the involvement of Russian regions in this process, and the formation of a national innovative economy that uses countries in the Asia-Pacific Region are actual and timely issues. These issues stimulate the finding of solutions that will allow for significant growth in the national economy and the importance of Russia in global society, a process that requires considerable analysis and conceptualization.

Chapter 2
Theoretical Aspects of Economic Growth in the Globalizing World

Abstract This chapter studies the conceptual foundations of economic growth in the globalizing world and conducts a problem analysis of "underdevelopment whirlpools" as an obstacle to economic growth. It describes the methodological foundations for the formation of a new concept of economic growth, and studies the philosophy of growth as a multi-disciplinary concept and an independent branch of the general theory of philosophy. The authors analyse the notion and sense of economic growth, determining its most important characteristics and the factors which build it, as well as determining the contradictions within economic growth and approaches to measuring it.

This chapter also determines the limits of economic growth, studies its interconnection with the notion of "economic development", and shows how to establish economic growth rate norms—a complex task that is especially relevant today—and determines their quantitative limits. The authors study the notion of "underdevelopment whirlpools" from the point of view of institutional theory, determine the mechanisms by which an economy is sucked into an "underdevelopment whirlpool", and how to overcome them. The authors also offer a model for calculating "underdevelopment whirlpools", study their dynamic nature, and map them throughout the world's developing countries.

2.1 Conceptual Foundations of Economic Growth in the Globalizing World

Economic growth is a key problem for macro-economic policy in all states. Developed countries, historically having provided a high level of income and stable gross domestic product (GDP) growth rates, are now being troubled with qualitative changes in economic growth, which are taking place under the influence of globalization and with social consequences for their populations. Developing countries face another problem—how to make the achievement of sustainable long-term growth rates based on a qualitatively new innovational basis one of the top priorities for state economic policy. Economic growth should be the foundation on which increasing living standards are built, creating the material basis for sustainable development, and guaranteeing equal participation of these countries in the global economic process, alongside developed countries.

The Russian economy has another problem as well: the key task is overcoming the system crisis that is related to transformation of the socio-economic system. Economic growth in Russia is unstable, and is based mainly on the situation in global raw materials markets; this was proved by the 2008 crisis. Economic growth, based on such factors, does not lead to increasing welfare for the whole population and does not ensure the growth of effectiveness and competitiveness in the national economy. Sustainability of the rate of economic growth in the long term is questionable as well. It is obvious that Russia has not formed a system of factors that guarantee dynamic rates of growth combined with the structural transformation of the national economy. In the globalizing world, Russia does not simply need quantitative economic growth but also requires a change in its quality, expressed in the innovational character of development, which would make Russian manufacturers more competitive in internal and global markets.

The methodological basis of the new quality of economic growth (NQEG) concept is the philosophy of growth. This is an independent branch of the general philosophy of economy, based on the main laws of dialectics; it encompasses all aspects of economic growth, with all of its contradictions, categories, and regularities. The philosophy of growth, using the classic categorical row (quality, quantity, leap, and measure) and fundamental laws, explains the processes that are taking place in the modern economy, builds causal relations, and allows analysis of the internal motivation of economic processes.

The philosophy of growth is part of the general theory of development, and is directly connected to the theory of evolution and to synergy. For the purpose of complex analysis, it is important to determine the touch and junction points.

The philosophy of growth, as an independent branch of the general theory of philosophy, is at the junction of philosophic, social, and economic sciences, and should use the corresponding categorical row and laws (Fig. 2.1).

The theory of evolution, which appeared after dialectics, is a sphere of theoretical natural science which has its own laws and uses its own scientific methods. Possessing specific features, it draws on materialistic dialectics. The union of philosophy and theoretical natural science is a necessary condition for the successful solution of various methodological problems. The data accumulated in various spheres of natural science could stimulate philosophical solutions of various problems.

The philosophy of growth and the theory of evolution differ as to their research objects (Table 2.1). The object of research in the modern theory of evolution is laws of development in the surrounding world and of the philosophy of growth—laws that relate to the development of the economic system.

Synergetics is a new direction in science, not related to the search for common laws of development that are applicable to both organic and non-organic systems. Synergetics is based on other principles, regarding its norms of order as strategic. Synergetics was first viewed as a science in the joint work of Haken and Graham, devoted to the study of lasers, in 1968. That was the start of the understanding of

2.1 Conceptual Foundations of Economic Growth in the Globalizing World

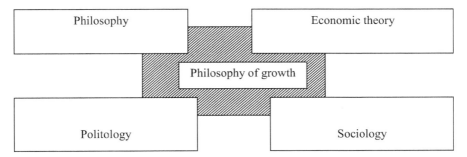

Fig. 2.1 Multi-disciplinary concept of the philosophy of growth (compiled by the authors)

Table 2.1 Connection between theories of development (compiled by the authors)

Parameters	Theories		
	Philosophy of growth	Theory of evolution	Synergetics
Object of study	Economic system	All surrounding world	Structure—attractors, as possible ways of development of material world
Main sphere of science	Philosophy; economics; sociology; politics	Theoretical natural science	
Key principle of systematization	Ordering		Complication
Principles of building the world	Simple out of the complex		All of the parts, complex out of the simple
Key factor of building the complex whole	Laws of public development	Natural selection	Chaos

synergetic, cooperative effects in the spontaneous formation of macroscopic structures, that is, self-organization.[1]

How successful the application of synergetics is to the description of behaviour of complex economic systems is a matter for debate. Observations through the prism of synergetics show only collective, mass processes in society, and the subjective choice of each economic agent, cooperation, motives, and behaviour cannot be discerned or explained.

Synergetics is based on unbalanced thermodynamics that study the birth of a complex and its genesis. The processes of chaoticization and simplification of

---

[1]Knyazeva E.N. Complex Systems and Non-Linear Dynamics in Nature and Society//Issues of philosophy.—1998.—No. 4—P. 140.

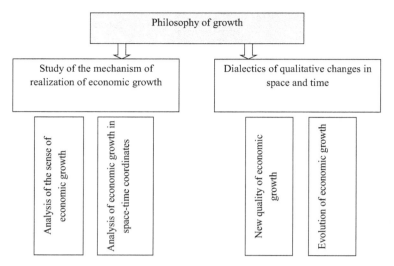

Fig. 2.2 Philosophy of growth (compiled by the authors)

organization are studied by synergetics only as evolutional stages in the functioning of the complex or as part of the journey to the more complex.[2]

The object of the research of synergetics is the structures–attractors of development. Synergetics allows us to forecast the processes based on their goals (structures–attractors) and general development tendencies of processes in integral environments, based on the desires and coordinated with the development tendencies of processes in these environments.

Economic growth, being an object of research into the philosophy of growth, integrates phenomenon and sense.[3] These categories are the most complex, but they are the most objective regarding the viewed process.

The philosophy of growth studies all issues related to the development of economic growth, such as phenomenon, sense, and process. The key directions of the philosophy of growth are shown in Fig. 2.2.

The phenomenon of economic growth is a simpler concept for philosophic analysis. It can be expressed in different forms, including relation, process, and structure. Like any phenomenon, economic growth has essential observability and apparency. These two features are related to the possibility of localizing economic growth in space and time. The space–time sense is indirectly related to recurrent processes of a similar nature in space and time. Taking this into account, economic growth of a specific country is both a manifestation of the individual and the similar. Possessing a unique individual nature, it may be compared to economic growth as a whole, which leads to a contradiction between the individual and the

---

[2]Knyazeva E.N., Kurdyumov S.P. Anthropic Principle in Synergetics//Issues of philosophy.—1997.—No. 3.—P. 62.
[3]Bogdanov Y.A. Sense and Phenomenon.—Kyiv, 1962.

recurrent. Economic growth, as a phenomenon, has a basis, or content, which differs from similar phenomena. The basis may be seen as a unification of the common and the specific. The basis of economic growth is labour, which has a lot of similar characteristics—for example, money relations, labour relations, and growth in the volume of production. The dialectical sense of economic growth consists of the fact that it embodies the systems of similar phenomena which have a common basis.

Economic growth is a comprehensive, organically connected system, all elements of which are equal, as some of them derive from each other, and some influence or are influenced by other elements. Successive connection of these elements and their subordination in a greater system are the structure of economic growth, which can be determined only by studying the system as a whole.

Analysis of the sense of economic growth is a necessary pre-condition for understanding its nature. In philosophy, "sense" is the totality of internally required relatively sustainable connections and relations in the material world which are the contradictory basis of a large diversity of phenomena. A "phenomenon" is the totality of different external attributes, connections, and relationships of an object, which determine its sense and the external forms of its existence. Economic growth is a dialectic integrity of sense and phenomenon. The gap between phenomenon and its sense leads to its subjectivization and the loss of its objective character.[4]

Economic growth is treated in economic science as sustainably growing change that results from the functioning of the national economy and the consumption of resources. The aim of economic growth is the growth in society's well-being. Economic growth means the progressive development of the economy; its progress. Factually, economic growth in terms of public production is manifested by the growth in volume of production of goods and services over a certain period. A criterion of quantitative evaluation of economic growth is usually the change of GDP in absolute value or per capita—as such, it is assumed that all GDP satisfies the needs of economic subjects.

Studying economic growth as a phenomenon, it is expedient to take into account the system of factors that influence the process of economic growth; the goals of economic growth; the type of economic growth; indicators of economic growth (its dynamics); and the contradictions of economic growth.

The most important characteristics of economic growth are the conditions that ensure the process of economic growth. They may have various characters, depending on the quality of economic growth.

The factors of economic growth are the foundations of the *process of growth*, as they largely determine the level and dynamics of changes, and influence the scale of increase in the volume of production, determine the type of economic growth, and increase the effectiveness of public reproduction.

The system of factors of economic growth is changed periodically in space–time, creating differences in rates, levels, and quality of economic growth. This

---

[4]Sense and Influence.—Kyiv: Naukova Dumka Publ. 1987.—P. 46.

situation is typical of a period of change in the key means of public reproduction, in the transformation of the economic system into a qualitatively new state. Thus, in the pre-industrial period, natural and geographic factors dominated, determining the natural and transformational type of economic growth. In industrial production, some factors in the former system lose their significance, while others undergo corresponding transformation. In addition, the system is supplemented by new factors which reflect the progress of production forces. The post-industrial age is an epoch in which there are qualitative changes in labour, when professional training becomes much more important, as does investment into human capital, with a special role belonging to competition and entrepreneurial capabilities, for example.

In other words, a systemic element of economic growth is the factor that directly or indirectly participates in the transformation of resources that go into the system. Direct participation is understood as direct influence of the factor on resources, while indirect participation supposes indirect influence through creation of common conditions for direct influence, such as legal, financial, and informational conditions. These factors are interconnected. Interfactorial relations are realized in material (product and energy) and information flows. Based on existing connections between the factors, their functions and the structure of economic growth are formed.

During an analysis of the sense of economic growth, it is important to note the contradictions which emerge as a result of struggle between various interests and goals.

Distinguishing the main contradictions that are peculiar to a certain object of research allows us to open and view the main content of the analysed process. Analysis of these contradictions helps to develop specific practical measures for solving and overcoming certain economic problems.

A special role in the contradictions in economic growth belongs to those contradictions that reflect the interconnection between nature and society. With the increase in the rates and scales of economic growth under conditions of scientific and technical progress, non-recoverable resources become scarcer and thus limit economic growth. Here there is a contradiction between unlimited growth of social and economic needs (interests and motives) and limited resources. The model of economic growth which exists at the moment holds a global threat to the natural balance of the Earth. But refusing to progressively develop the economy may also lead to unfavourable consequences. Solving these contradictions is possible by harmoniously integrating the economic and ecological policies of a state.

One of the main contradictions of economic growth is also a contradiction between consumption and accumulation. This appears when growth of the share of national income used for consumption reduces the possibility of accumulation that ensures future consumption. In its turn, excessive growth of the accumulation share hinders the current satisfaction of needs, which might lead to a decrease in living standards. In order to solve this contradiction, it is necessary to determine and realize the most favourable balance between them. Under the conditions of a market economy, averaging out contradictions between accumulation and consumption is somewhat complicated, as a private/capitalistic form of ownership supposes the independence of market subjects in selecting how to use their received income. In this case, state regulation is widely used.

The next contradiction is also born from scientific and technical progress. It relates to the provision of full employment under the conditions of perfecting the material means of production. Application of more efficient equipment leads to a gradual reduction of need for human resources, which threatens the policy of full employment. This problem could be solved through involvement of the workforce in new production or by the state's use of the population for state enterprises, public works, or in the service sphere.

Special attention should be paid to socio-economic contradiction between production and consumption. Production and consumption are connected by the reproduction process, but they differ by their characteristics and by the conditions in which these processes take place. Firstly, they differ in the level of cognition and forecasting. Secondly, there are differences from the point of view of possibilities of influence on these two sides of the reproduction process. Thirdly, the time factor plays different roles in production and consumption. Even if a very short period of time is taken—when it could be considered that production does not change at all—consumption will not remain a fixed value. Fourthly, even the time spent in the processes of production and consumption is evaluated differently.

Economic growth, as a complex phenomenon, has many quantitative and qualitative indicators which characterize not only economic but also social results. Among these indicators the most important are absolute increase of real GDP, GDP and national income over a certain period, and, even more important, increases in real GNP (gross national product), GDP, and national income per capita over a certain period. Both indicators could be used. For example, if attention is paid to the problems of economic and military and political potential, the first group of indicators is more suitable. For comparison of living standards of population in specific countries and regions, it is preferable to use the second group of indicators. Thus, Indian GDP exceeds Swiss GDP by 70 %, but in living standards India is behind Switzerland by more than 60 times.

The simple measurement of economic growth, which is often understood as all it entails, is really the tip of an iceberg. The rate of economic growth does not have any essential evaluation. To say that $n\%$ is economic growth is to say nothing. Economic growth has a base which, increasing or decreasing, determines economic climate in space–time.

Economic growth contains a range of determinations: qualitative and quantitative, space and time. These determinations are also the abstract limitations of economic growth (Fig. 2.3). Quantitative limits are expressed within the limits of rates of economic growth, which emerge because of two reasons: the quantitative limit of economic growth is related to the limitation of economic possibilities and to institutional limitations, such as norms of economic behaviour: limitations caused by society's transition to sustainable development with corresponding activities of public organizations being oriented towards the protection of nature.

Fig. 2.3 Limits of economic growth (compiled by the authors)

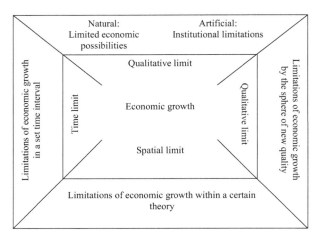

An example of institutional limits of economic growth would be an institution which does not allow economic growth to go beyond the formed limits of quantitative indicators. For example, international financial institutes, while conducting foreign economic policy in the interests of developed countries, can restrain the process of sustainable growth in developing countries. Qualitative limits differ from other limits by the fact that going beyond them means a leap into a new state, characterized by a new measure.

Economic growth consists of the dialectic interaction of the internal content of the object ("object in itself") and its external manifestation ("object for another"). As an "object in itself", economic growth has a certain set of characteristics: factors, contradictions, and basis. As an "object for another", economic growth exists not independently but has relationships with other objects. In other words, economic growth is inseparable from public reproduction, being its result.

An important aspect of analysis of economic growth is its interconnection with the notion of "economic development". In our opinion, it is necessary to differentiate "economic growth" from "economic development". Firstly, development takes place when there is not growth but certain preconditions for it exist. Secondly, it could be expressed in structural transformations and various innovations which do not lead directly to economic growth. Schumpeter understood economic development as "creation of new (or creation of new quality) good, implementation of a new method (means) of production, mastering of new sales market, receipt of new source of raw materials, conduct of corresponding reorganization (for example, provision of monopolistic position or elimination of monopolistic state of another enterprise)".[5] Thirdly, development could take place along the line, when there is no quantitative growth, but instead a process of reduction of attributes and qualities of products and services.

---

[5]Schumpeter J. Theory of Economic Development: (An Inquiry Into Profits, Capital, Credit, Interest, and the Business Cycle).—M.: Progress, 1982.—P. 159–169.

2.1 Conceptual Foundations of Economic Growth in the Globalizing World

Economic growth provides economic development, but it doesn't replace it. Therefore, from the point of view of interconnection of the processes of development and growth of the economy, development is a category at a higher level. In other words, economic growth is only a "manifestation" of development, one of its scenarios or variants.[6] "As economic growth becomes the goal of state policy, economists do not percept development without economic growth. Meanwhile, development—in its true sense—is the change of the system on the whole, transition from one qualitative state to another."[7] Myrdal states that "development is treated as progressive movement of the whole social system".[8] "Progressive movement" is not economic growth, fixed by measurements of macro-items, but the increase in the level of satisfaction of the main needs of all members of society—primarily, by means of the growth in well-being of the poor. In this regard, it is obvious that main needs can be satisfied only through the process of economic growth.

The above circumstances allow us to conclude that economic growth, *in a narrow sense*, is a process in which interaction of the system of exogenous and endogenous factors, which is born at the stage of direct production, acquires a sustainable character at other stages of public reproduction, leading to quantitative and qualitative changes in production forces, an increase in public product over a certain period, and the growth of public well-being.

In a wide sense, economic growth is a reflection of existing economic and institutional conditions which determine—together with other indicators—the direction of movement of society, setting the character of public development as progressive, regressive, or inertial. As an object of research in the theory of development, economic growth has qualitative and quantitative determination. Its substance appears through analysis of the unity of qualitative and quantitative characteristics; it possesses the features of continuity and discretization (the presence of one or another attribute is determined by time and space determination); and with each new level, it crosses the "limits" of the old state and acquires a new quality, which is a regular process of internal transformations of the economic system, the result of acquisition of new forms, features, and attributes based on the constant accumulation of certain quantitative stock, and measures in economic and social components.

Quality of economic growth includes determination (external side) and systematicity (internal side), which indicates certainty. Economic growth is determined by limit, finiteness, and attributes, and systematized through elements and structure. Qualitative distinguishing of growth as an object of research is fundamental for achieving cognitive certainty on this issue. "First, there come

---

[6] Aleksandrova E.N. System of Factors of Economic Growth of National Economy: PhD thesis: 08.00.01.—Krasnodar, 2004.—P. 11–23.
[7] Sukharev O. Modern Tendencies of Economic Development//Economist.—2003.—No. 7.—P. 30–45 (p. 35).
[8] Myrdal G. Asian Drama. An Inquiry into the Poverty of Nations.—N.Y., 1996.—189 pp. (p.18).

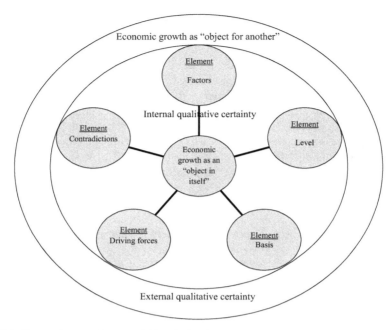

Fig. 2.4 Economic growth as an "object in itself" and "object for another" (compiled by the authors)

impressions, and then there is something,—then go notions 'quality' (definition of an object or phenomenon) and 'quantity'."[9] Quality supposes integrity, as it is not just a sum of attributes but a totality of interactions of various aspects of the viewed phenomenon (Fig. 2.4).

"Quality–quantity" analysis is an inseparable part of the NQEG concept. The key identification differs from the qualitative by the scale and level of manifestation of the distinguished attribute. Quantity is determination or the sum of single-qualitative objects. Quantity, separated from qualitative diversity, integrity and sustainability, includes the whole set of the objects or phenomena which possess this quality. When we speak of the quantitative notion "rate of economic growth", we suppose that qualitative processes have appeared.

The category "quantity" is closely related to the category "value", which denotes the objective quantitative side of any object, attribute, or ratio. A separate value is an element of a certain system, and the value of this element is pre-determined by the structure of this system and relations of a certain kind. Measurement of homogeneous attributes provides a system of measurement of homogeneous values. For example, the system of measurement of economic growth includes a set of

---

[9]Timofeev I.S. Methodological Purpose of Categories "Quality" and "Quantity".—M., Nauka, 1972.

indicators that are interconnected and are a part of the system of national accounts (SNA).

The balance between quality and quantity is so conventional that even such state of economy as "economic growth at the level of 2 %" could be viewed from either the qualitative or the quantitative side: 2 % quantitative determination has its quality, as the words "more" and "less" can be applied to it.

There is a contradiction between quality and quantity, which consists of the fact that quantity is subject to comparison (as qualitative manipulation) to another value or number, but can exist beyond this comparison. Besides, quantity that differs from quality through a lack of diversity has a qualitative component, as it is a set of single-qualitative objects; and, with the accumulation of its own lack of diversity, it leads to the appearance of a new measure and a new quality.

As economic growth changes qualitatively in each moment in time, there appears a contradiction between continuous qualitative transformation and the single-quality of its attributes and characteristics. There is differentiation between qualitative changes for levels of influence. As an "object in itself", economic growth could be measured as a lot of time, but as an "object for another", it changes not with each change of level but with the change of the measure.

In reality, qualitative manifestations are set by quantitative parameters and there is neither quantitatively uncertain quality nor qualitative manifestations of uncertain quantity. Each qualitative element could be measured quantitatively, and this quality is differentiated by limits—the measure. Determination of the measure for qualitative transformation of economic growth as an "object for another" is pre-determined by internal contradiction of economic growth, its continuity, and its heterogeneity. That is why measurement of a measure during transition to a new quality will always have a subjective character based on retrospective data.

An important direction of the study of economic growth is consideration of it through theoretical and multiple notions that are abstracted from the qualitative nature of the elements of multitudes. Of course, there is functional dependence of attributes of economic growth on surrounding influence. But complexity and contradiction of economic growth are manifested in the fact that while changing the level of material well-being, it changes itself into a new qualitative state. This happens automatically through changes in the qualitative measure of a national economy's efficiency.

Changing measures of efficiency could be observed with the help of the data provided by Angus Maddison in his book *The World Economy: a Millennial Perspective*,[10] where he systematized quantitative changes in the global economy, beginning in 1000 AD (Table 2.2, Fig. 2.5).

While the level of economic growth constituted thousands of dollars in the past, now it constitutes millions of dollars. This difference is substantial, but it is not about digits, rather about the change in the measure, which includes a significant

---

[10] Maddison A. The World Economy: a Millennial Perspective/Development Centre of the Organization for Economic Co-operation and Development.—2001.

Table 2.2 Level of GNP per capita in countries of groups A and B over 1000–1998 (in USD on the 1990 exchange rate)

States	Years				
	1000	1500	1600	1700	1820
On average for group A (Western Europe and neighbouring countries, Japan)	405	704	805	907	1130
On average for group B (Latin America, Eastern Europe, Asia (excluding Japan and Africa))	440	535	548	551	573

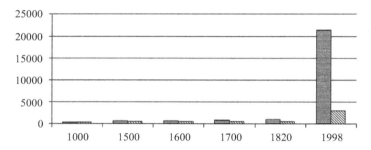

▣ For group A on average (Western Europe and neighboring countries, Japan)

▨ For group B on average (Latin America, Eastern Europe, Asia (excluding Japan and Africa))

Fig. 2.5 Change of the measure of quantitative efficiency of national economy

qualitative substance. Each growth of the measure means the growth of material well-being of each member of the society and the growth of his possibilities and potential.

"Norm" is a category that is methodologically close to the measure. Unlike the measure, the norm is a process and a category used in all spheres of life. As a philosophical category, a norm is movable, changing, contradictory, conventional, and relative. The norm receives its practical expression in normative behaviour.

What is normal economic growth? This question is not as simple as it may appear at first. Setting it pre-supposes a certain methodological trap. The connection of normal and abnormal states was studied by antique science, but as philosophy developed, the volume of new knowledge grew and old postulates and axioms were put into doubt—including those regarding the pre-determinacy of harmony as a totality of norms.

Determining normatives (the practical manifestations of a norm) of a rate of economic growth is a complex task, especially so today. Determination of quantitative limits of economic growth is an attempt to invade the limits of normality. But these limits have space–time boundaries, so they are relative and conventional.

Besides, these limits pre-determine interests which may not coincide, and public, corporate, and private interests in the process of their dialectical interaction could correct the limits of normalization that are set by the external amorphous (e.g., scientific) environment.

The limits of normalization may be set by an individual, corporation, or state. But normatives are set by formal institutes. It is possible to speak of the norm under the influence of changes in the measure. This means that the measure is not just a means through which the norm is presented, but an institutional limitation of its possibilities. A measure, being a harmony of quantitative and qualitative substances, stimulates the change into a new qualitative state, thus setting its conditions for a space–time interval.

For example, in the age of globalization, the number of mergers and acquisitions was measured in the thousands, and the measure "thousand" indicates not just transnationalization but the beginning of a new globalization, which is considered in Chap. 4.

Each step of history means movement to a new measure and new complications of essential characteristics. A norm lies within the new measure, and is a range of optimal functioning for an object or a system.

2.2 Problem Analysis of "Underdevelopment Whirlpools" as Obstacles for Economic Growth

Countries that began their economic movement earlier have progressed—and not only in gross national income. They won time, and occupied the main global market niches. "An important peculiarity of modern competition is harsh aggravation of struggle for leadership. In this context, scientific and technical research is formed in order to occupy the positions, ensure the establishment of standards convenient for the leader, and register patents, thus ensuring additional income of companies—in particular, through quick growth of capitalization of its assets".[11]

Polarization of the global economy led to the establishment of "underdevelopment whirlpools", which are a system of space–time circles of development, along which the countries move, overcoming the barriers of "vicious circles of poverty" and trying to find their niche in the international division of labour.[12] "Underdevelopment whirlpools" hinder developing countries from entering the modern global society as equal partners. Moreover, they are a reason for international isolation and the strengthening of dualism not only within a country but also in the international arena. "Underdevelopment whirlpools" emerge under the pressure

---

[11]Kollontay V. Western Concepts of Economic Globalization/M.S. Gorbachev et al. Levels of Globalization: Difficult Issues of Modern Development.—M.: Alpina Publisher, 2003.—592 p.

[12]Compiled by the authors based on the materials: Bolotin B. World Economy over 100 Years// World Economics and International Relations.—2001.—No. 9.—P. 98.

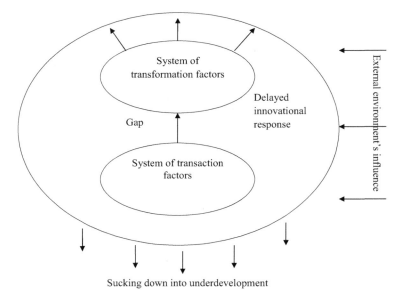

Fig. 2.6 Mechanism of being sucked down into "underdevelopment whirlpools" (compiled by the authors)

of expansion of the developed states, which thus create conditions for economic and political hegemony, stimulating the appearance of additional possibilities for their development, measured by the growth in GNP (or GDP) per capita.

Using the instrument of the thoroughly axiomatized multi-factor theory of Inshakov, it is possible to determine the nature of "underdevelopment whirlpools" as developing countries lose their chance to form the system of transaction factors owing to time underrun and the necessity for increasing the system of transformation factors for innovation that respond to the influence of a quickly developing external environment.

The only way out of the excessively globalized "underdevelopment whirlpools" is by creating the emergence of new circles of development that are based on new innovational cycles. A feature that is peculiar to a new quality of economic growth is the establishment of a new innovational cycle which projects and creates additional circles of development (Fig. 2.6).

From the point of view of institutional theory, the viewed phenomenon is characterized as "institutional traps" or "effects of blocking", which are "ineffective sustainable norms (institutes) with self-reproducing character".[13]

"Institutional traps" exist in various spheres of the economy: in property relations, money and monetary systems, the real sector of the economy (industry), etc. At the same time, most of the traps, viewed theoretically, do not have a dynamic

---

[13]Polterovich V.M. Institutional Traps and Economic Reforms.—M.: RES, 1998.

2.2 Problem Analysis of "Underdevelopment Whirlpools" as Obstacles...

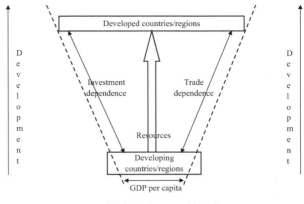

Fig. 2.7 Process of being sucked down into "underdevelopment whirlpools" (Popkova 2010b)

component—economic growth is viewed regardless of the rates of development of leading countries and regions. As a result, the goals of development have overpowered its character, and do not take into account perspective changes in levels of economic growth and, therefore, competitiveness of particular states and regions, as compared in the future.[14]

Overcoming these obstacles is possible by using the "underdevelopment whirlpools" idea. "Underdevelopment whirlpools" reflect a mechanism in which particular regions or states lose possibilities for development because of an underrun in time and the necessity to oppose the negative influence of globalization (Fig. 2.7).

In the most complicated cases, such chronic underrun leads to the final loss of possibilities for development owing to intensive outflow from states or regions of all types of resources—labour resources in the form of migration, capital, natural resources as a finite source of extensive development, and entrepreneurial capital in the form of brain drain.

The content analysis of such a phenomenon as an "underdevelopment whirlpool" requires determination of its parameters: its depth and speed. The depth of this theoretical "whirlpool" could be measured by the time underrun of a developed country, using, in particular, the map of time asymmetry. The speed of the whirlpool is a more complex parameter, as it is a dynamic process. A theoretical model of the whirlpool involves the process by which the effectiveness of transformational factors (human, technical, and natural) are reduced—in other words, striving for zero in the ratio of limiting results to limiting costs:

---

[14]Popkova, E.G. "Underdevelopment Whirlpools" as a Tool of Spatial and Temporal Measurement of Economic Development/E.G. Popkova, T.N. Mitrakhovich//Journal of International Scientific Publication: Economy and Business.—2011.—Vol. 5, Part 1.—P. 298–306.—Eng.

$$V = \partial R / \partial C => 0 \tag{2.1}$$

where V—speed of being sucked into a whirlpool; ∂R—limiting result from investment of transformation factors (industrial result); ∂C—limiting investments of transformation factors.

The closer V is to zero, the quicker is the process of being sucked into a whirlpool (Table 2.3).

For the purpose of calculating these parameters, GDP per capita of the analysed region is compared with GDP of the developed territory/region. If GDP of the developed territory/region is lower, it is necessary to calculate the depth of the "underdevelopment whirlpool" and the speed at which an economy is sucked into it.

Depth is determined by comparing the underrun over the two viewed successive time periods. Speed is calculated by dividing the whirlpool's depth by the time interval between two successive dates of analysis. An economic sense of the depth of "underdevelopment whirlpools" consists of the number of years by which the territory is behind over the studied time period, and the speed shows how this underrun increases annually.

Analysis of the dynamics of intercountry disproportions, performed in the previous part, allows us to build a map of "underdevelopment whirlpools" for specific countries (Fig. 2.8).

The dynamic nature of "underdevelopment whirlpools" is manifested by the presence of unique "pulsations" in the speed of underrun—in some years the speed of underrun grows, in others it reduces, which may be caused by the appearance of favourable conditions in which existing production factors may be used. At the same time, it is necessary to note that in the globalizing world this underrun could be caused by a more negative influence of global economic crises on economies that are in an "underdevelopment whirlpool", as they are objectively weaker and dependent on the international situation owing to weak internal demand.[15]

In the 1970s, the foreground of scientific discussions was occupied by the theory of advantages of lagged development. This was built on the hypothesis that less developed societies have advantages which allow them to surpass a more developed society in the future. The followers of this theory observed that societies which were pioneers in the development of new technical and economic systems sometimes have to pay a large price for these novelties (for the cost of research and development). However, the most important thing was that they became dependent on large investments in the initial stages of technology development. Their lagged rivals did not have to invest in development and research—they simply accepted the new forms and technologies after they appeared.

---

[15]Popkova, E.G. "Underdevelopment Whirlpools" as Instrument of World Economy Polarization Measurement/E.G. Popkova, L.S. Shakhovskaya, T.N. Mitrakhovich//Global Business and Economics Anthology.—2010.—Vol. I, March.—P. 304–309.—Eng.

2.2 Problem Analysis of "Underdevelopment Whirlpools" as Obstacles...

Table 2.3 Model of calculation of "underdevelopment whirlpools"[a]

Name of country/region	GDP^{Y_1}c^j	Y_GDP$_{C\text{-developed}}$	$Y_1 - Y\_GDP_{C\text{-developed}}$	GDP^{Y_i}c^j	Y-GDP$_{C\text{-developed}}$	$Y_i - Y\_GDP_{C\text{-developed}}$	D	Speed	GDP^{Y_m}c^j	Y_GDP$_{C\text{-developed}}$	$Y_m - Y\_GDP_{C\text{-developed}}$	D	Speed
C^1													
C^2													
...													
C^j													
...													
C^n													

Notes
1. C^j—name of country/region, where $j = 1\ldots n$
2. GDP^{Y_i}c^j—GDP per capita of the country C^j, where Y_i—years of calculation of underrun from developed countries, where $i = 1\ldots m$
3. $Y\_GDP_{C\text{-developed}}$—year when GDP per capita of the country C^j (from previous column) coincides with GDP per capita of the developed country
4. D—change of the depth of "underdevelopment whirlpools" in studied intervals of time, $D = (Y_i - Y\_GDP_{C\text{-developed}}) - (Y_{i-1} - Y\_GDP_{C\text{-developed}})$
5. Speed—speed of being sucked into "underdevelopment whirlpool", Speed $= D/(Y_i - Y_{i-1})$

[a]Popkova (2010c)

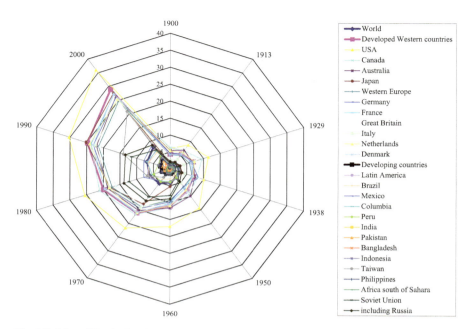

Fig. 2.8 Map of "underdevelopment whirlpools" of developing countries of the world. [Compiled by the authors on the basis of *World Economy: Global Tendencies over 100 Years*/Ed. by I.S. Korolev.—M.: Economist 2003.—604 p. (appendices pp. 493–602)]

Torstein Veblen pointed out that Germany and USA overtook England in the late nineteenth/early twentieth centuries, and Lev Trotsky considered that the Soviet Union would gain profit from the so-called "law of unequal and combined development". Most discussions regarding the advantage of slow development are focused on industrial ages and the leadership of rivals in the global economy. But the theory is much wider. History has examples of societies that were leaders in development at first but were overtaken by other, underdeveloped, societies. Let us recall the fates of Sumer, Babylon, Assyria, Egypt, Persia, Athens, and Rome—states with high levels of development in their times. The same fate could meet highly developed societies whose positions are unstable; and less developed societies could overtake them.

This hypothesis leads to one of the most important and interesting issues in the whole sphere of economic development: how can an underdeveloped society overcome a developed society?

The hegemony of developed countries is expressed not only in the level of accumulated material wealth but in the level of generation and distribution of new knowledge and the formation of a system of transactional factors. Technological novelties, which are the foundation of national wealth for post-industrial states, cannot be effectively produced or copied—and in some cases cannot be used in industrial, let alone agrarian, societies. Meanwhile, the need for these novelties is rather high, for progressive development is possible only if they are used as a basis. This is the root of the most important reason for the recent expansion of the gap between the developed countries of the West and all other countries of the world.[16]

By the early 1990s, seven leading post-industrial states possessed 80.4 % of global computer equipment, controlled 87 % of the registered patents, and provided 90.5 % of high-tech production. The volumes of export of American intellectual property grew 3.5 times between 1986 and 1995, and the positive trade balance in this sphere constituted more than $20 billion. By 1995, the USA accounted for three-quarters of the world market of information services and services for data processing, the volume of which constitutes $95 billion at the time of writing. The inflow into developed countries of huge financial resources, which was not accompanied by a reduction in the volume of intellectual property that remained with their citizens, allowed an increase in the rates of scientific and technical revolution. During the 1990s, the countries that are members of the OECD spent $400 billion on average at 1995 prices on scientific R&D. Today, the USA alone accounts for 44 % of global expenses for these purposes, while the countries of Latin America and Africa together provide less than 1 %; the number of scientific and technical employees for each million of population constitutes 126,200 in the USA, while the average global indicators do not exceed 23,400. Private American corporations spend around $30 billion annually to increase the educational level of their employees, which is equal to the total expenses for all scientific research in Russia, China, South Korea, and Taiwan.[17]

Gerschenkron developed a theory according to which the character of modern economic growth (particularly in Europe) changes with the level of economic underrun over time.[18] The time underrun should be discussed only regarding the age of economic growth—that is, from the late sixteenth century. Of course, it is possible to speak about a more or less high development of a certain nation (state) in the earlier ages. However, under the conditions of total stability and lack of significant socio-economic or technological changes over a long period of time, measured in centuries, the problem of overcoming underdevelopment was solved very easily—by simple adaptation of the achievements of a more developed nation by a less developed one. A decisive role in this belonged to conquests: for example, the Romans borrowed a lot from conquered Greece and then passed their culture to Barbarians. But when there is economic growth which changes the living conditions of each generation of people, a developing country should not just develop but develop *quicker than the leading one*. Besides, it does not suffice to adapt the achievements of the latter, as such a method will fix the gap—it is necessary to find

---

[16]Inosemtsev V.L. Technological Progress as Fundamental Basis of Social Polarization/Megatrends of Global Development.—M.: Economics, 2001.—P. 26–58.

[17]See previous reference.

[18]Economic theory. Transformation Economics: Study Guide/I.P. Nikolaeva, L.S. Shakhovskaya, E.G. Popkova [et al.]; ed. by I.P. Nikolaeva.—M.: UNITI-DANA, 2004.

mechanisms that are unknown to the more developed country. This is the main rule—it is impossible just to follow the path of a more developed country.

Starting conditions of the country that is lagging behind create two sources of tension: one of them is a wish to close the gap in income with regard to the most developed countries; another is the greater difficulty in growing the economy owing to scarcer (poorer) preliminary conditions for growth, as compared to the starting point for the leading countries. As the underrun of a country increases, so the tension grows as well. Tension leads to impatience, which leads to decisive, radical, and even revolutionary steps in all spheres—economic, political, and social. Impatience and various preliminary conditions lead to particular paths of economic growth. An example is the choice that is made when economic growth starts with industrialization but changes to agriculture are postponed. An advantage that compensates for certain difficulties in developing countries is the possibility of borrowing technologies from developed countries without the expensive and time-consuming process of developing them from scratch.

Dynamism in the Western counties is born not from the necessity for making a response to an external challenge and not by internal contradictions of post-industrial society; rather, it embodies the potential of a creative personality, human self-realization as a quality—according to Marx "a measure of all things" under the conditions of the information economy.[19] This is the main guarantee for the fact that such development cannot be turned back. Surely, it is more complex—as compared to industrial development. And, since all countries that want to develop consider quick industrialization, it becomes obvious that the task of overtaking the post-industrial world cannot be achieved with industrial methods.[20]

---

[19]Davis S., Meyer C. Future Wealth.—Boston (Ma.), 2000.—P. 40.

[20]Inozemtsev V.L. Limits of Overcoming Development (Series: Economic Problems at the Brink of Centuries).—M.: Economics, 2000.—295 p.

Chapter 3
Foreign Trade as a Vector of Economic Growth in the Globalizing World

Abstract This chapter views theoretical aspects and the evolution of the establishment of international trade, as well as determining the role of foreign trade in the development of national economies under modern conditions. The authors analyse various definitions of the notion "trade", determine the role of trade in the sectorial structure of gross domestic product (GDP), study the definitions of the notion "service", view the main characteristics of internal trade and the structure of foreign economic activities, and determine the methods of organization of foreign trade and the most significant types of risks in foreign trade.

The authors also study the processes of globalization, the deepening of internationalization of economic life, transnationalization, the appearance of a large number of international organizations and integration associations, and the development of foreign economic relations in general and foreign economic contacts in particular. The chapter views the theory of closed and open economies, and the sense of tariff and non-tariff limitations, analyses the history of the establishment of international economic relations, and the policy of import substitution, as well as determining the main pros and cons of the model of export orientation. The authors study distinctive features of the modern global economy, study dynamics of foreign trade turnover in selected countries, dynamics of export and import, trade balance, GDP and GDP per capita, changes in export and import quotas, direct foreign investments, and the number of transnational corporations.

3.1 Foreign Trade: Theoretical Aspects and Evolution of Establishment

Trade is one of the fastest evolving spheres of economic life, the evolutional development of which is rooted deep in history. Trade is one of the first spheres of the economy, forming as a result of the natural division of labour in society (internal trade) and was one of the first forms of international economic relations, the primary goal of which was solving the questions related to providing goods that were limited in availability or absent from the national market (being part of foreign trade).

Despite the obvious significance of internal and foreign trade, most attention was paid to the latter. This was because of the necessity for providing state regulation of this sphere in order to preserve national interests. As a result, the accumulated theoretical knowledge about foreign trade is very rich now. Nevertheless, we should remember that it is impossible to speak of foreign trade in isolation from internal trade. On the one hand, it is obvious that these two spheres of activities solve different tasks and perform different functions—especially now that geo-political factors play a large role in intercountry relations. On the other hand, the nature of the two types of trade is identical, or develops in step: success in foreign trade is possible only when national internal trade policy is built wisely.

Analysis of economic literature shows that there is no significant scatter of opinions regarding the notion "trade" or "trade activities". Historically, the notion of "trade" was used in the widest meaning of the word, and included all economic activities around the buying and selling of goods and services.

According to the definition given in the *Large Soviet Encyclopedia*, "trade is a sphere of national economy providing turnover of commodities and their movement from the production sphere into the sphere of consumption" (Popkova and Tinyakova 2013c). "In a narrower sense, 'trade' is purchase of commodities and their sale without implementation of substantial material changes. In its turn, trade between several countries, consisting of import and export of products, is foreign trade; trade between different countries in its totality is international trade" (Popkova and Tinyakova 2013c) (Table 3.1).

Despite an obvious specific character of activities and "exchange", in view of the sectorial structure of gross domestic product (GDP), trade is usually related to the service sphere (Fig. 3.1).

Table 3.1 Definitions of the notion "trade"

Term	Notion	Source
Trade	Sphere of economy and type of economic activities, the object of which is turnover of goods, buy and sell of products, and servicing buyers in the process of selling the goods and their shipment, storage of goods, and their preparation for sales	Dictionary Borisov A.B. Economic Dictionary.—M.: Knizhny Mir, 2003.—895 p
Internal trade	Sphere of economy which realizes goods in the internal market of the country	Dictionary Borisov A.B. Economic Dictionary—M.: Knizhny Mir, 2003.—895 p
Foreign trade	Trade with other countries, export of goods from countries, and import of goods into the country	Rayzberg B.A., Lozovskiy L.S., Starodubtseva E.B. Modern economic dictionary. 5th edition.—M.: INFRA-M, 2007.—495 p
International trade	Totality of trade connections and foreign trade relations of the states that trade with each other	Dictionary Borisov A.B. Economic Dictionary—M.: Knizhny Mir, 2003.—895 p

Note: compiled by the authors on the basis of the sources: Edward (2012), Popkova et al. (2013d)

3.1 Foreign Trade: Theoretical Aspects and Evolution of Establishment

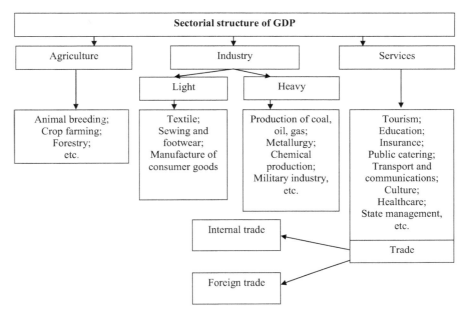

Fig. 3.1 Role of trade in sectorial structure of GDP. *Note*: compiled by the authors on the basis of the sources: Popkova (2013)

In this case, we deem it important to emphasize one of the special characters of trade, as opposed to other types of services. This is that production and provision of services is impossible without trade, while production and presence of products can be separated in time and space from corresponding trade operations.

Building on the definition of service, it is possible to see that from a terminological point of view the notions "services" and "trade" are not equal (Table 3.2).

On the one hand, trade—like all other types of services—is a group of activities that bring benefit, not a certain item. However, on the other hand, it is the only service that performs a unique function of exchange. If services are generally an object of trade, they are, as a matter of fact, a mechanism of exchange. International practice already has an agreement regarding the understanding of the term "service"—"all objects of trade that are not goods" (Popkova et al. 2013a).

In other aspects—primarily in characteristics—specifics of services and trade coincide. Trade is peculiar for its invisibility, intangibility, variability in quality, inseparability of production and consumption, and its impossibility of storage.

Based on the country to which the members of trade activities belong, trade is divided into internal and foreign trade.

Internal trade is a sphere of economy that realizes commodities in the internal market to redistribute goods and services according to consumers' needs. It started when the growth of the urban population began to complicate direct contacts between manufacturers of final products and consumers. Beginning at that time, the volume of internal trade grew constantly, and in the nineteenth century, as rapid

Table 3.2 Definition of the notion "service"

Author	Definition	Source
A. Smith	Service is "intangible" goods, consumed and disappearing in the moment of production	Smith A. "An inquiry into the nature and causes of the wealth of nations". L.: Gossocekgiz, 1935. V.2. 475 p
K. Marx	"This expression means nothing else but the special consumer value provided by labor—like any other commodity; but special consumer value of this labor received specific name "service", because labor provides services not as an item but as activities"	Marx K., Engels F. Works. 2nd Edition. V. 26. P. 1. P. 413
S.I. Ozhegov	Service is an action that brings benefit and help to another person, or creation of conveniences provided to someone	Ozhegov S.I., Shvedova N.Y. Russian Definition Dictionary. M., 1999. P. 476
A.N. Rodnikov	Service is a special type of products that satisfies public and private needs	Rodnikov A.N. Logistics: Terminological Dictionary. M., 2000. P. 147
T. Hill	Service is implementation of changes into a state of a person or commodity, coordinated between two persons	Hill T.P. On goods and services. Review of Income and Wealth. Vol. 23 (December 1977). P. 315–338

Note: compiled by the authors on the basis of the sources: Othman et al. (2014), Popkova and Tinyakova (2013c, d), Wamboye and Adekola (2013), (Hill 1977)

development of cities and industry took place, internal trade expanded, allowing for connections between manufacturers and consumers.

As a result, the main goal of internal trade became obvious: "It was considered that the sense of trade consisted in exchange—in reality, it consists in making a product more accessible to a consumer", which was characterized by Say in his work *Study of political economics* (Klinov 2015).

The role of internal trade is not limited just by material distribution of products. It stimulates production and sets a certain direction, according to the demands of consumers and influences the effectiveness of the market economy (Scott 2012).

As was mentioned above, it is impossible to speak of foreign trade in isolation from internal trade, so it is necessary to understand the foundations and causes of this process (Fig. 3.2).

As to its forms of organization, internal trade is divided into wholesale (aimed for further resale within the country or purchase of raw materials for production processes) and retail (purchase of small shipments of products or separate shipments). However, it should be noted that this division is not applied to its external direction. For that, it is necessary to bear in mind that the practice in Russia and in countries with transitional economies included small-scale wholesale foreign trade as shuttle trade, and nowadays trade via internet stores is very popular throughout the world.

Regarding the definition, foreign trade is generally treated as activities through which deals are performed in the sphere of goods, services, information, and intellectual property.

3.1 Foreign Trade: Theoretical Aspects and Evolution of Establishment   29

Preconditions of internal trade expansion:

↓

1. Quick development of craft and manufacture production which led to deepening of the processes of specialization.
2. Growth of merchant capital.
3. Growth of urban population which hindered direct contacts between manufacturers and consumers of material goods, etc.

↓

Main strategic goal of internal trade
Development of adequate organizational and legal mechanism of bringing commodities to a consumer, which provides positive development of internal market on the whole

↓

Main functions of internal trade:

↓

1. Realization of manufactured consumer value (goods). Performance of this function creates an economic precondition for reproduction of total public product and connects production to consumption.
2. Taking consumer products to consumers. Trade ensures space transportation of goods from manufacturers to consumers; trade includes processes of production in the sphere of turnover (namely, transporation and storage).
3. Supporting the balance between offer and demand. At the same time, trade inf luences production in the issues of volume and assortment of manufactures goods.
4. Reduction of costs of turnover in the sphere of consumption (consumers' expenses for purchase of goods) by improvement of the technology of sales, information services, etc
5. Functions related to implementation of marketing, namely: market research, determination of price, creation of service departments, development of goods, etc

---

Fig. 3.2 Main characteristics of internal trade. *Note*: compiled by the authors on the basis of the sources: Delgado et al. (2012), Klinov (2015), Maswana and Farooki (2013)

Foreign trade is one of the directions of foreign economic activities (FEA),[1] together with international technical, economic, and investment cooperation, and cooperation in the sphere of monetary, financial, and credit operations (Fig. 3.3).

It pre-determines continuation of the process of creating products for the internal market. Taking goods abroad, the country finds additional sales markets, thus providing full potential for its created products. In other words, if internal trade operations are not optimized in the country, the results of foreign trade activities cannot bring maximum profit to national participants.

If foreign trade is viewed not from the position of its national participants (companies and their intermediaries) but from the position of the country, when

---

[1] It is necessary to distinguish the notions "foreign economic connections" (FEC) and foreign economic activities (FEA). FEC are forms of realization of interstate relations on the part of scientific and technical, production, and trade cooperation, and monetary and financial relations. FEA are conducted at the level of production structures (forms, organizations, enterprises, associations, etc.) with full independence in the choice of foreign market and foreign partner, nomenclature, and assorted positions of goods for export–import deals, in determining price and cost of contract, volume and terms of shipment, and is a part of their production and commercial activities with internal and foreign partners.

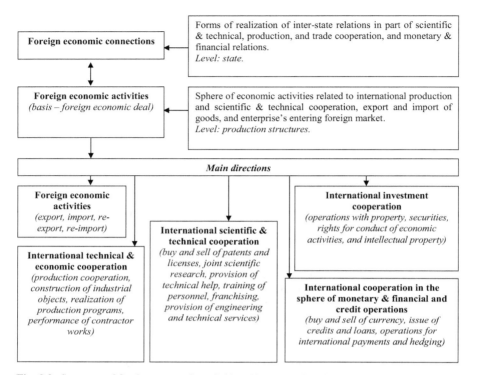

Fig. 3.3 Structure of foreign economic activities. *Note*: compiled by the authors on the basis of the sources: Maswana and Farooki (2013), Popkova and Tinyakova (2013a), Popkova et al. (2013c)

the subject of trade operations is the state, it is possible to distinguish several main methods of its performance (Table 3.3).

It should be noted that despite a wide range of methods by which international trade may be conducted, only two of them are currently popular: direct and indirect methods, together with a combination of various methods. In the first case, direct connections are established between a manufacturer (supplier) and final consumer. In the second, the presence of an intermediary link is pre-supposed.

Analysis of theoretical developments in the conduct of foreign trade operations shows that the most important issues in the theory of international trade are the search for reasons for its conduct and the optimization of a country and commodity structure for export/import.

The first systemic studies aimed at solving these issues were the works of mercantilists in the sixteenth–eighteenth centuries, in which they came to the conclusion that in order to receive gold in the international market it was necessary to expand export and reduce import. The lack of theory is obvious—if all countries export goods, which countries will import them?

3.1 Foreign Trade: Theoretical Aspects and Evolution of Establishment

Table 3.3 Methods of organization of international trade

Method	Main characteristics	
Direct export (import)	Export of products from the country of production into the country of consumption according to the concluded (without an intermediary) international trade deal	
Indirect export (import)	Export of products from the country of production into the country of consumption according to the concluded (with an intermediary) international trade deal	
Cooperative export (import)	Export of products from the country of production into the country of consumption according to the concluded (using a special intermediary, without whom performance of the deal is impossible, risky, and/or economically ineffective) international trade deal	
Countertrade	Trade operations, during conclusion of which obligations for conduct of counter purchased of goods or services for full or partial cost of the goods arise between the exporter and the importer	
International auctions, trading, stock, and fairs	Public trade operations, conducted on a competitive basis with the help of specialized institutes	
International lease	Operative lease—provision of the object of lease for a term smaller than the item's lifecycle and incomplete amortization of equipment for the rental term, with further prolongation of contractual term of rental or return of the equipment to the leasing company	Financial lease—provision of the object of lease for the long-term within the indirect method (three-sided character of the deal) with payment of the full cost of amortization of the equipment or its greater part, and additional costs of the leasing company
	International lease is divided into direct and indirect. Direct international lease, depending on the directions of the movement of the object of lease, is divided into export and import	
	Export lease—lease contract, according to which domestic lease company transfers the objects of lease to foreign leaseholder	Import lease—lease contract, according to which foreign lease company transfers the object of lease to domestic leaseholder

Note: compiled by the authors on the basis of the sources: Popkova et al. (2013a, c)

It is considered that in the late eighteenth and early nineteenth centuries representatives of the classic school of political economics, prominent English economists Smith and Ricardo, formulated the theoretical foundations of international trade. In particular, the latter proved that foreign trade for any country is always profitable, but export operations should not involve all goods but only those in which the country has a relative advantage, expressed in high labour efficiency.

After this, the classical ideas were supplemented and developed by representatives from other schools of economic analysis. The most interesting are ideas about the optimization of foreign trade operations, offered by Leontyev, Vernon, Kindleberger, and Porter, for example.

Analysis of the accumulated creative knowledge about the conduct of trade operations shows that international trade is obviously a more complicated sphere of economic life than internal direction: it includes more expensive deals (in view of taxes and charges); and it is more risky, as goods cross borders all over the world.

Foreign trade differs from internal trade in the following respects:

- It is slower;
- It is limited in the range of goods and services offered in the market;
- It is influenced by a lot of risk factors.

Generally speaking, a high risk level for operations is the most significant difference between foreign trade and internal trade.[2] In particular, while it is easier to track non-payers in internal trade, and the laws in one's own state might help to solve the problem quickly, the same scenario in foreign trade might cost more money, time, and effort.

The most significant types of risk in foreign trade are the following (Popkova et al. 2013c):

- Political risks relating to political instability in the country;
- Commercial risks related to a changing cost of the commodity after the contract is signed; to mistakes in preparation of documents or payment for products; to transportation or refusal to accept products;
- Inflation risks caused by reduction of cost of funds owing to inflation processes;
- Liquidity risks emerging owing to the impossibility of buying or selling the funds quickly or in necessary quantity;
- Credit risks caused by a debtor's non-payment of debt and irregular service of debt;
- Investment risks caused by depreciation of invested financial assets and ineffectiveness of expression of investment projects;
- Reserve risks emerging owing to change of prices or moral ageing;
- Interest risks, expressed by a sudden change in bank interest rate;
- Currency risks, expressed by a sudden change in foreign currency rates.

The real significance of risks in foreign trade pushes its members (companies and countries alike) to search for adequate tools for its regulation. As a result, the role of supranational institutes and organizations grows significantly: every year, the number of countries in various financial, economic, and trade organizations grows.[3]

It should be noted that under modern conditions, international organizations play a very important role in solving significant international issues and are an addition to traditional contractual relations between countries, which allows international

---

[2]Risks in foreign trade—attitude of investor to the possibility of making or losing money.

[3]At present they include, for example, Asian Pacific Economic Cooperation (APEC), Consumers International (CI), European Bank for Reconstruction and Development, EurAsEc, the European Free Trade Association, the World Trade Federation, the World Customs Organization, the International Chamber of Commerce, and the World Trade Organization (http://russian.people.com.cn/31519/8180469.html).

3.1 Foreign Trade: Theoretical Aspects and Evolution of Establishment

cooperation to take place on a completely new basis (Popkova and Tinyakova 2013a).

In addition, it is necessary to emphasize that activities undertaken by these structures have been taking place and significant for a very long time, and their appearance is a regular step in the evolutionary development of trade: its expansion and complication. History tells us that trade organizations of an intergovernmental nature have been appearing since the mid-nineteenth century, when they were organizations with a narrow sphere of activities.[4]

We consider that we should look much further back for the roots of modern intergovernmental trade organizations. In the twelfth to the seventeenth centuries, the Hanse Trade Union functioned in order to protect trade and merchants from feudal lords and pirates in Northern Europe. In the early nineteenth century, the German Customs Union functioned. All the states governed by this union obeyed the same laws regarding import, export, and transit of goods, for example.

By analysing the evolution of foreign trade, it is possible to see that it is nothing new. It first appeared in the period of transition from a primitive communal system to the slave-owning system, by means of the beginning of labour division and the emergence of commodity–money relations. Foreign trade appeared in slave-owning and feudal societies, where a natural economy was dominating. However, initially it didn't cover all product groups and served the aristocracy and ruling circles. The global market began to appear at the moment when feudal society began to decay. An obvious push towards the development of international trade took place during the so-called Age of Discovery.

Later on, the transformation and complication of foreign trade operations were related to the processes of regionalization, integration, transnationalization, and, of course, globalization. As a result, foreign trade did not remain single trade deals, but developed into long-term full-scale trade and economic cooperation, which then grew into international trade and began to influence the development of national economies more and more.

---

[4]Including the International Association of Geodesy (1864), the International Telecommunication Union (1865), the World Meteorological Organization (1873), the Universal Postal Union (1874), the International Bureau of Weights and Measures (1875), the International Association for Protection of Industrial Property (1883), the International Association for the Protection of Literary and Artistic Works, (1886), the International Union of Railways (1886), and the International Union for Printing Customs Tariffs (1890). Unlike the previous institutional forms of interstate communication (international conferences, commissions, and committees), international administrative unions had operating bodies (so called "international bureaux"), though, on the whole, their organizational structure was rather weak (Delgado et al. 2012; Popkova & Tinyakova 2013a).

3.2 Role of Foreign Trade in the Development of National Economies in the Modern World

Owing to the development of globalization processes, the deepening of the internationalization of economic life, transnationalization, and the appearance of various international organizations and integration associations, almost all countries of the world became equally involved in foreign economic relations, in general, and participants in foreign trade contacts, in particular.

Back in the fifteenth–eighteenth centuries, when capitalistic relations were emerging, theoretical and practical economists started searching for the sense of foreign trade, its purposes and causes of existence. However, there was no issue regarding countries' participation in foreign trade contacts. It was clear that while there was unlimited growth of human needs and limited resources, foreign trade had to be conducted, as it was one of the methods by which states could enrich themselves.

Later, in the eighteenth–twentieth centuries, searching for the answers to the questions "How one should conduct foreign trade wisely?" and "What's to be sold and what's to be purchased?", specialists formulated the development of state foreign trade policy. Taking into account the availability of natural resources in the country, level of labour efficiency, volume and quality of production factors, the presence of highly qualified labour resources, effectiveness of entrepreneurship, conditions of demand, and so on, it is necessary to understand that the main criterion of a country's participation in foreign trade activities was still prices. "Not simply the prices, but the ratio of internal and foreign prices. Brazil sells coffee, Saudi Arabia sells oil, and Japan sells computers because under the existing ratio of internal and world prices, manufacturers and suppliers from these countries receive profit by selling their products to foreigners (world market prices are higher than internal prices). At the same time, it's more profitable for Japan to buy Brazilian coffee and Saudi oil, and for Brazil and Saudi Arabia to buy Japanese electronics for the same reason—own production of the imported products would be more expensive" (Delgado et al. 2012).

At present, understanding the causes behind the appearance and development of global markets in goods, services, production factors, and scientific and technical progress, and observing the increasing involvement of countries in the formation of demand and offer for them, specialists name liberalization as an essential modern characteristic of the markets and the subjects which form them. The increase in freedom in the processes of international movement of "traded" goods and services, and the reduction in state interference in the development of foreign trade policy determine the current commodity and country structure of the world markets.

It should be noted that inclination towards the policy of free trade might have both a voluntary and a mandatory character. In the first case, striving for the conduct of trade without limitations appears to indicate a high level of development in the country's economy and its competitiveness, when expansion of alternative offer for the goods manufactured by domestic companies will stimulate the deepening of the country's specialization and development of its national economy. In the second case, conducting the policy of free trade might be related to the establishment of new rules and terms for the game that do not always correspond to the level of economic development of the country; when, for example, the country becomes a member of an international economic organization or a participant in an integration association.

Theoretically, the level of openness of the country in foreign trade and the level of its foreign economic liberalization may vary and be set for each country or member of an international economic organization individually, on the basis of the use of tariff and non-tariff limitations by the state.

According to the statistics, distribution of non-tariff limitations among the developed countries has an obvious tendency towards reduction. Thus, for example, the share of non-tariff limitations (calculated as % of import) in the USA for 1988–1996 reduced from 16.7 % to 7.7 %, and in Japan—from 8.6 % to 7.4 % (Maswana and Farooki 2013). However, when compared with tariff limitations, their significance grows owing to an increase in the total volume of international trade and the expansion of commodity assortment in the global market (Popkova et al. 2013c).

It should be noted that the use of tariff and non-tariff limitations not only characterizes the level of "freedom" of countries in the global markets but also provides an idea of the level of maturity of a national economy, which can be determined on the basis of the model of development of foreign trade used by the state: export-oriented or import-substituted. In this case, there is a contradiction between a policy of free trade and a policy of protectionism.

Analysing the history of the establishment of international economic relations, we see that a policy of import substitution was topical while economies were developing industrially. The strategy of import substitution was first used by the USA and the countries of Western Europe in the early 1850s to support national industry. It received a further boost in the 1950s–1960s when the countries of Latin America, to protect themselves from expansion by their northern neighbours, took some measures to reduce prices for domestically produced goods and to modernize national industry. This approach was also successful in the countries of Asia and Africa.

In the 1970s–1980s, the policy of import substitution was criticized. The thing is that for many countries import-substituting industrialization led to the creation of ineffective enterprises, protected from foreign competition and with weak or absent competition in the internal market. Instead of limiting imports and reducing protectionism, import substitution was used in all spheres of national economies, which led to the creation of enterprises whose products were manufactured in comparatively unfavourable conditions (http://russian.cri.cn). As a result, a reduction of the level of competition in the internal market led to a reduction in the effectiveness of national economies. In addition, the use of this model is very doubtful from the point of view of optimal use of global resources and the creation of new jobs.

Today, developed and many developing countries (primarily new industrial countries) stick to the policy of export orientation. It is considered that the

Table 3.4 Main advantages and disadvantages of the model of export orientation

Advantages	Disadvantages
1. Active use of "given by nature" comparative advantages with the further possibility of creation of competition	1. Dependence on situation at the global markets where the growth of trade barriers is possible owing to strengthening of pricing competition
2. Active balance of payment leads to inflows of foreign currency into the country which might and should be used for development of own spheres and creation of new jobs	2. Weak protection of domestic consumers In case of problems with shipment of the leading export products, the economy might face a crisis: lack of currency inflow, problems in the internal market of capital, growing internal debt, termination of production, barter exchange, etc.
3. Increase of employment, reduction of unemployment Growth of volumes of production leads to increase of demand for labour and influences positively the growth of wages	3. Cancellation or reduction of currency control measures and control over capital turnover may lead to national economy's vulnerability against speculators' attacks
4. Growth of population's income, more equal distribution of income among representatives of various professions and between city and village	4. Complexity of search for own niche in the global markets. Tough competition Multi-sectorial economy is required for the country to enter its specialization in the process of international division of labour. Or an absolute advantages is required, which cannot be copied by rivals
5. Possibility of using the effect of scale If internal market is not large enough for obtaining economy from the scale effect, this effect could be achieved from entering the external markets by means of export products	

Note: compiled by the authors on the basis of the sources (http://russian.cri.cn)

development of the economy is provided by means of investments, aimed at development of the local sector of the economy and stimulating the creation of new jobs. Thus, with the growth of the population's income, there is an increase in the size of the internal market (Knyazeva 1998). According to the UNCTAD (United Nations Conference on Trade and Development) experts, the top priority for the development of foreign trade is the development of the economy's export spheres: increase of export of goods and services leads to an increase in their production, putting into operation the new production capacities, and the creation of new jobs (Доклад секретариата Конференции ООН по торговле и развитию 1987).

It should be noted that despite the more complex character of the policy of export orientation, it corresponds to a rather high level of national economy development. As well as obvious advantages, it has some drawbacks, which could be opposed without using economic autarky (Table 3.4).

It is understandable that owing to the presence of players in the global markets with different levels of economic development, increasing the level of openness of some of them should lead to protection of manufacturers by some and the use of elements of a protectionist policy by others. However, this does not happen openly. On the one hand, countries try to coordinate the processes of regulation of their

3.2 Role of Foreign Trade in the Development of National Economies in the...

foreign trade relations through concluding two-way deals and multi-way agreements of regional character and using the help of multi-way global conventions. On the other hand, owing to membership of international economic organizations (primarily the WTO—the World Trade Organization) or integration groups, they often have to play according to the common rules. If, for example, liberalization is undertaken, it is undertaken everyone.

Features of the modern global economy include its openness and deepening processes of liberalization, when there is annual growth in the dependence of countries on the state of world markets where they supply their goods and services and where they purchase products for internal consumption. Not a single economy in the world can stay away from these processes. Moreover, the higher indicators of export and import for countries, the more they are dependent on the level and quality of development of their foreign trade relations.

Using the statistics, it is possible to see that the countries which are most dependent on the global markets and which often most influence the situation within them include not only such developed states as the USA, Germany, France, Japan, UK, and Italy, but also the developing economies of China, Russia, India, and Brazil, whose total share in the global commodities turnover constitutes around 50 %. A peculiar fact is that as to dynamics, the developing export-oriented economies showed the largest growth rates in their foreign trade turnover. In particular, as compared to 1990, the volume of foreign trade turnover of China grew by 41.3 times by 2014, India by 15.7, Brazil by 6.6, and Russia by 4.3, while in France, Japan, Germany, and the USA the corresponding indicator grew only by 2.3–3.4 times (Table 3.5).

In particular, as at year-end 2014, the first place for volume of exports belongs to China—12.3 % of the global volume of export, the USA accounts for 8.5 %,

Table 3.5 Dynamics of foreign trade commodity turnover of selected countries, $ billion

No.	Country	1990	1995	2000	2005	2010	2014	Share of the global foreign trade turnover, %
1	China	104.1	282.5	474.4	1422.0	2973.0	4301.7	11.3
2	USA	1181.8	1714.5	2038.7	2636.8	3247.0	4033.1	10.6
3	Germany	851.5	1182.8	1054.3	1743.7	2336.0	2723.2	7.1
4	Japan	610.4	893.5	858.7	1109.8	1464.0	1506.1	4.0
5	France	545.6	698.6	603.5	958.1	1127.0	1260.3	3.3
6	UK	511.1	664.5	621.1	893.0	966.0	1189.8	3.1
8	Italy	430.6	538.6	474.3	747.0	932.0	1000.5	2.6
7	Russia	186.6	218.2	150.7	368.9	649.0	805.8	2.1
9	India	49.7	82.4	92.8	229.9	547.0	784.6	2.1
10	Brazil	70.1	123.3	113.6	195.9	393.0	464.3	1.2
	Other	4224.0	2632	6550.9	10,908.9	16,005.0	20,023.8	52.6

Note: compiled by the authors on the basis of the sources (http://www.wto.int)

Table 3.6 Dynamics of export of selected countries, $ billion

No.	Country	1990	1995	2000	2005	2010	2014	Share in global exports, %
1	China	57.4	147.2	249.3	762.0	1578.0	2342.3	12.3
2	USA	552.1	811.9	781.1	904.4	1278.0	1620.5	8.5
3	Germany	425.2	598.9	551.5	969.9	1269.0	1507.6	7.9
4	Japan	319.3	482.9	479.2	594.9	770.0	683.8	3.6
5	France	267.3	360.9	298.1	460.2	521.0	582.6	3.1
6	Italy	216.6	291.0	237.8	367.2	448.0	528.7	2.8
8	UK	246.8	335.5	284.1	382.8	406.0	505.8	2.7
7	Russia	93.9	115.8	105.2	243.6	400.0	497.8	2.6
9	India	22.6	39.1	42.3	95.1	220.0	321.6	1.7
10	Brazil	37.9	55.8	55.1	118.3	202.0	225.1	1.2
Other		2112.4	1280.2	3280.3	5532.6	8145.0	10,186.3	53.6
The world		4351.5	4519.2	6364.0	10,431.0	15,237.0	19,002.2	100.0

Note: compiled by the authors on the basis of the sources (http://www.wto.int)

Germany 7.9 %, Japan 3.6 %, France 3.1 %. As compared to 1990, China's exports grew by 40.8 times, India's 14.2 times, Brazil's 5.9 times, Russia's 5.3 times, and Germany's 3.5 times (Table 3.6).

These states supply to the global market the main share of industrial products and food and ensure distribution of new technologies, as well as providing a wide range of services.

In their turn, in volume of global imports, as at year-end 2014, the USA accounted for 12.6 %, China 10.3 %, Germany 6.4 %, Japan 4.3 %, and France 3.5 %. Compared to 1990, China's imports grew by 41.9 times, India's 17 times, Brazil's 7.4 times, USA's 3.8 times, and Russia's 3.3 times (Table 3.7).

These countries are the main importers of raw materials and semi-finished products to provision their production complexes and manufacture export products.

As of year-end 2014, a positive trade balance was observed with China ($383.0 billion), Germany ($291.1 billion), Russia ($189.7 billion), and Italy ($57.0 billion). The other studied countries had a negative trade balance, which shows negative tendencies in the development of their economy and a change in their status from creditor to debtor (Table 3.8).

Having said that, it is necessary to remember that a positive trade balance is not the one and only criterion for a highly effective macro-economic policy. Rather, it is an important factor in stimulating the inflow of foreign investments. A key factor which plays a strategic role in determining the investment attractiveness of the state is a readiness to conduct reforms that will change the structure of the economy (Popkova and Tinyakova 2013a).

Concluding the statistical material on a rather wide spectrum of indicators which characterize the level of involvement of countries in world trade, it is possible to

Table 3.7 Dynamics of imports of selected countries, $ billion

No.	Country	1990	1995	2000	2005	2010	2014	Share of the global imports, %
1	USA	629.7	902.6	1257.6	1732.4	1969.0	2412.5	12.6
2	China	46.7	135.3	225.1	660.0	1395.0	1959.4	10.3
3	Germany	426.3	583.9	502.8	773.8	1067.0	1215.7	6.4
4	Japan	291.1	410.6	379.5	514.9	694.0	822.3	4.3
5	UK	264.3	329.0	337.0	510.2	560.0	684.0	3.6
6	France	278.3	337.7	305.4	497.9	606.0	677.7	3.5
7	Italy	214.0	247.6	236.5	379.8	484.0	471.8	2.5
8	India	27.1	43.3	50.5	134.8	327.0	463.0	2.4
9	Russia	92.7	102.4	45.5	125.3	249.0	308.0	1.6
10	Brazil	32.2	67.5	58.5	77.6	191.0	239.2	1.3
Other		2111.6	1351.8	3270.6	5376.3	7860.0	9838.0	51.5
The world		4414.0	4511.7	6669.0	10,783.0	15,402.0	19,091.0	100.0

Note: compiled by the authors on the basis of the sources (http://www.wto.int)

Table 3.8 Dynamics of trade balance of selected countries, $ billion

No.	Country	1990	1995	2000	2005	2010	2014
1	China	10.7	11.9	24.2	102.0	183.0	383.0
2	Germany	−1.1	15.0	48.7	196.1	202.0	291.9
3	Russia	1.2	13.4	59.7	118.3	151.0	189.7
4	Italy	2.6	43.4	1.3	−12.6	−36.0	57.0
5	Brazil	5.7	−11.7	−3.4	40.7	11.0	−14.0
6	France	−11.0	23.2	−7.3	−37.7	−85.0	−95.1
7	Japan	28.2	72.3	99.7	80.0	76.0	−138.4
8	India	−4.5	−4.2	−8.2	−39.7	−107.0	−141.4
9	UK	−17.5	6.5	−52.9	−127.4	−154.0	−178.1
10	USA	−77.6	−90.7	−476.5	−828.0	−691.0	−792.0

Note: compiled by the authors on the basis of the sources (http://www.wto.int)

state that the same countries are constant leaders. The main reason is obvious—the largest scale organization of foreign trade contacts has been achieved by the largest economies of the world: large production means large sales and large purchases. Ten economies provide around 60 % of the world GDP, with a significant share for China, 16.6 %, and the USA, 16.0 %. In 1990–2014 China showed high growth rates—its GDP grew by 16.4 times (Table 3.9).

The reverse connection is of great interest: if the volume of industrial production determines the level of a country's involvement in global trade, doesn't state policy for foreign trade have an impact on the economic development of the country? It surely does. "In our times, even the largest and richest country of international exchange and foreign trade ... requires the provision of decent and normal human

Table 3.9 Dynamics of GDP (PPP—purchasing power parity) of selected countries, $ trillion

No.	Country	1990	1995	2000	2005	2010	2014	Share of world GDP, %
1	China	1.1	2.2	3.6	6.5	12.1	18.0	16.6
2	USA	6.0	7.7	10.3	13.1	15.0	17.4	16.0
3	India	1.0	1.4	2.1	3.3	5.4	7.4	6.8
4	Japan	2.4	2.9	3.3	3.9	4.3	4.6	4.2
5	Russia	1.2	0.8	1.0	1.7	2.9	3.7	3.4
6	Germany	1.5	1.9	2.2	2.7	3.2	3.7	3.4
7	Brazil	1.0	1.3	1.5	2.0	2.7	3.3	3.0
8	France	1.0	1.2	1.6	1.9	2.3	2.6	2.4
9	UK	1.0	1.2	1.6	2.1	2.3	2.6	2.4
10	Italy	1.0	1.2	1.5	1.7	2.1	2.1	1.9
Other		11.2	14.6	19.1	26.0	35.4	43.1	39.7
The world		28.4	36.4	47.8	64.9	87.7	108.5	100.0

Note: compiled by the authors on the basis of the sources (http://www.worldbnk.org)

existence". Living standards cannot be improved without that. "It is necessary to use favorable conditions and apply all factors and resources in order to satisfy human and society's needs fully, better, and in a more reliable way" (Popkova and Tinyakova 2013a).

Statistics confirmed this conclusion. Ranking the countries as to significance of exports and imports in the creation of GDP is of some interest. Comparing the indicators that characterize the change ratio of export and import to GDP (export and import quotas) to indicators of living standards, we see the following picture. Over 1970–2014, the change of export quota in the analysed countries had a "pendular" character from the 1980s to the 1990s (Italy, Germany, UK, USA, Japan, South Korea, Brazil, and China).

As was mentioned above, the leaders for the cost of export in 2014 were China, USA, Germany, Japan, and France. For these countries, the value of export quota constituted: for Germany 45.7 %, France 28.7 %, China 22.6 %, USA 14.8 %, and Japan 9.3 %. The leading countries for this indicator over the last 50 years have been Hong Kong (219.6 %), Luxembourg (203.3 %), and Singapore (187.6 %). As compared to 1990, the largest growth of export quota was observed with China, 3.3 times, Luxembourg, 2.0 times, and Germany, 2.0 times (Table 3.10).

The values of these indicators show that, on the one hand, the leading countries mentioned above have wide possibilities for production and sales of national goods and services in the global market (this could be expensive high-quality products and consumer goods of low price). On the other hand, the high value of the export quota could be explained not so much by the volumes of exports as by cost of export products and the volume of internal markers, as well as the inability to consume large volumes of issue of products from any spheres of the national economy, which restrains (without possibility of export) the development of these spheres. In the case of Russia, it is possible to speak of the weak development of processing spheres, which do not need the volume of products of extracting spheres.

3.2 Role of Foreign Trade in the Development of National Economies in the... 41

Table 3.10 Dynamics of change of export quota of selected countries, %

Countries	1970	1975	1980	1985	1990	1995	2000	2005	2010	2014
Hong Kong	93.2	83.4	88.9	107.2	130.7	142.9	141.8	194.7	219.4	219.6
Luxembourg	90.4	94.0	90.0	110.3	100.4	105.2	148.3	162.1	180.7	203.3
Singapore	126.1	137.1	202.1	152.4	177.2	181.2	189.2	226.1	199.3	187.6
Malaysia	41.4	43.0	56.7	54.1	74.5	94.1	119.8	112.9	93.3	73.8
South Korea	12.9	25.3	30.2	29.8	25.9	26.7	35.0	36.8	49.4	50.6
Germany	15.2	17.2	18.7	23.0	22.9	22.0	30.9	37.8	42.3	45.7
Russia	–	–	–	–	18.2	29.3	44.1	35.2	29.2	30.0
Italy	15.2	18.8	20.2	21.2	18.3	24.7	25.6	24.6	25.2	29.6
France	15.8	18.7	20.8	23.1	20.8	22.4	28.2	26.4	26.0	28.7
UK	21.3	24.9	26.0	27.3	22.6	27.2	26.3	25.8	28.7	28.4
India	2.5	4.8	6.0	8.9	15.9	20.4	20.7	33.7	26.2	23.2
China	3.7	5.5	6.0	5.2	6.9	10.7	12.8	19.3	22.0	22.6
USA	5.5	8.2	9.8	7.0	9.2	10.6	10.7	10.0	12.4	14.8
Brazil	7.0	7.5	9.1	12.2	8.2	7.4	10.2	15.2	10.7	11.5
Japan	10.6	12.5	13.4	14.1	10.3	9.1	10.9	14.3	15.2	9.3

Note: compiled by the authors on the basis of the sources (http://www.worldbnk.org)

A similar picture is observed in the dynamics of the development of imports: a reduction in the share of imports in GDP was observed in the 1980s–1990s (France, Germany, Italy, Japan, South Korea, Malaysia, Brazil, and India). For example, in Singapore, which enters the top three countries for the corresponding indicator, the share reduced from 209.0 % to 152.1 % in 1980–1985. In Luxembourg, which was ranked third as of year-end 2014, the share reduced from 91.6 % to 83.2 % in 1985–1990. In view of the rate of its growth, it is possible to see that in 1990–2014 the largest growth in import quota was observed in India (3.1 times increase), Luxemburg (2.1 times), and Brazil (2.0 times) (Table 3.11).

It should be noted that in the 1980s–1990s the analysed countries showed a reduction of the key indicator of living standards—GDP per capita. For example, in China this indicator reduced from $318 to $298 (against the background of a reducing share of exports); in Germany from $11,747 to $9125 (reduction in the share of imports); in Japan from $42,847 to $36,172 (reduction of both exports and imports); in UK from $9625 to $8214 (reduction of the share of imports); in Italy from $8218 to $7712 (reduction of the share of imports); in Russia from $3837 to $1768 (reduction of the share of imports) (Table 3.12).

In its turn, such countries as India and Brazil show—as a result of high growth rates of GDP, growth of cost of exports (by 2 times), and imports (by 2.5 times) in 2005–2010—show a quick growth of GDP per capita: in India from $735 to $1370 and in Brazil from $4743 to $10,993. In 2010–2014, this tendency was preserved in these countries. The picture wouldn't be complete without mentioning the dynamics of the viewed indicators in the countries of Southeast Asia with an export-oriented model of macro-economic development. Thus, over 1970–2014, GDP per

Table 3.11 Dynamics of changes of import quota of selected countries, %

Countries	1970	1975	1980	1985	1990	1995	2000	2005	2010	2014
Hong Kong	85.5	77.8	89.4	97.1	122.1	147.4	137.4	182.4	213.5	219.6
Luxembourg	67.1	78.1	79.0	91.6	83.2	80.3	121.6	135.4	147.1	170.9
Singapore	145.1	146.5	209.0	152.1	167.1	164.5	176.9	196.3	172.8	163.2
Malaysia	37.3	42.5	54.3	49.1	72.4	98.0	100.6	91.0	76.3	64.6
South Korea	22.5	33.3	37.6	29.2	26.9	27.7	32.9	34.4	46.2	45.3
Germany	16.6	18.9	23.3	25.1	23.1	21.5	30.6	32.7	37.1	39.0
France	15.3	17.7	22.4	23.5	21.6	20.9	27.1	26.8	27.9	30.5
UK	20.4	26.4	23.8	26.1	24.3	26.7	28.3	28.4	31.1	30.3
Italy	15.0	18.7	22.8	21.6	18.1	21.1	24.8	24.8	27.1	26.5
India	3.8	6.5	9.1	7.5	8.3	11.8	13.7	22.0	26.3	25.5
Russia	–	–	–	–	17.9	25.9	24.0	21.5	21.1	22.9
China	2.5	4.9	6.6	13.9	13.7	18.1	18.7	29.2	23.2	18.9
Japan	9.4	12.6	14.4	10.8	9.4	7.7	9.4	12.9	14.0	17.8
Brazil	7.4	11.5	11.3	7.1	7.0	9.3	12.4	11.8	11.8	14.3
USA	5.2	7.3	10.3	9.6	10.5	11.8	14.3	15.5	15.8	13.8

Note: compiled by the authors on the basis of the sources (http://www.worldbnk.org)

Table 3.12 Dynamics of GDP per capita (current prices, $ thousand)

Countries	1970	1975	1980	1985	1990	1995	2000	2005	2010	2014
Luxembourg	4.5	9.1	17.3	13.1	35.0	53.4	49.0	79.5	103.3	116.7
Singapore	0.9	2.5	4.9	7.0	11.9	24.9	23.8	29.9	46.6	56.3
USA	5.2	7.8	12.6	18.3	24.0	28.8	36.4	44.3	48.4	54.6
Germany	2.8	6.2	12.1	9.4	22.2	31.7	23.7	34.7	41.8	47.8
UK	2.3	4.3	10.0	8.7	19.1	21.3	26.4	40.0	38.3	46.3
France	2.9	6.7	12.7	9.8	21.8	27.0	22.5	34.9	40.7	42.7
Hong Kong	1.0	2.3	5.7	6.5	13.5	23.5	25.8	26.6	32.6	40.2
Japan	2.0	4.6	9.3	11.5	25.1	42.5	37.3	35.8	42.9	36.2
Italy	2.1	4.1	8.4	8.0	20.8	20.6	20.1	32.0	35.9	34.9
South Korea	0.3	0.6	1.8	2.5	6.6	12.4	11.9	18.7	22.2	28.0
Russia	–	–	–	–	3.5	2.7	1.8	5.3	10.7	12.7
Brazil	0.4	1.1	1.9	1.6	3.1	4.8	3.7	4.7	11.1	11.4
Malaysia	0.4	0.8	1.8	2.0	2.4	4.3	4.0	5.6	9.1	11.3
China	0.1	0.2	0.2	0.3	0.3	0.6	1.0	1.7	4.5	7.6
India	0.1	0.2	0.3	0.3	0.4	0.4	0.5	0.7	1.4	1.6

Note: compiled by the authors on the basis of the sources (http://www.worldbnk.org)

capita in Hong Kong grew from $963.0 to $40,169.5, in Malaysia from $343.0 to $11,307.1, and in Singapore from $925.0 to $56,284.6 (http://www.worldbnk.org).

In our opinion, another interesting fact is the interconnection between activity of the country in foreign trade operations and its investment attractiveness, which

3.2 Role of Foreign Trade in the Development of National Economies in the... 43

Table 3.13 Dynamics of DFI, new inflow (current prices, $ billion)

Countries	1970	1975	1980	1985	1990	1995	2000	2005	2010	2014
China	–	–	–	1.7	3.5	35.8	38.4	111.2	243.7	289.1
USA	1.3	2.6	16.9	20.0	48.5	57.8	321.3	138.3	259.3	131.8
Hong Kong	–	–	–	–	–	–	61.9	41.0	82.7	116.0
Brazil	–	1.3	1.9	1.4	1.0	4.9	32.8	15.5	53.3	96.9
Singapore	0.1	0.3	1.2	1.0	5.6	11.5	16.5	18.1	55.1	67.5
UK	1.5	3.3	10.1	5.5	33.5	21.7	122.2	253.7	66.7	45.5
India	–	–	0.1	0.1	0.2	2.1	3.6	7.3	27.4	33.9
Russia	–	–	–	–	–	2.1	2.7	15.5	43.2	22.9
Italy	0.6	0.6	0.6	1.1	6.4	4.8	13.2	19.6	9.9	13.7
Malaysia	0.1	0.4	0.9	0.7	2.3	4.2	3.8	3.9	10.9	10.6
South Korea	–	–	0.0	0.2	0.8	1.8	9.3	13.6	9.5	9.8
Japan	–	–	0.3	0.6	1.8	0.04	8.2	5.5	7.4	9.1
Germany	–	0.7	0.3	0.8	3.0	12.0	210.1	59.9	86.1	8.4
France	0.6	1.6	3.3	2.6	13.2	23.7	42.4	88.8	38.9	8.0
Luxembourg	–	–	–	–	–	–	–	6.6	38.6	7.1

Note: compiled by the authors on the basis of the sources (http://www.worldbnk.org)

could be determined by the indicator of new inflow of direct foreign investments (DFI).

Real numbers show that investment attractiveness of the country cannot depend only on the level of its economic development. In particular, the volume of DFI in China as of year-end 2014 was larger than in the USA, and in Brazil it was larger than in France, Italy, Japan, or UK. A major role in its formation belongs to the level of openness of the country in foreign economic relations. Thus, significant increase in the inflow of DFI into China (from $38.4 to $111.2 billion) was observed in 2000–2005; into France, Italy, Japan, South Korea, Singapore, UK, and the USA after 1995 (Table 3.13). In these periods, the countries opened their markets for foreign partners, entering the WTO.

A direct result of the growth of DFI volumes into the country is a change in the structure of the reproduction process, in which a significant role belongs to transnational corporations (TNCs).

There are more than 70,000 TNCs in the world at the time of writing. According to UNCTAD data, most of them are in the USA (806 companies), UK (531), Canada (374), Australia (312), Germany (286), and Russia (201) (Table 3.14).

According to the data published in *Fortune* magazine, the largest TNCs are in the USA (132 companies), China (73), Japan (68), France, and Germany (32 each).[5]

---

[5]They include Royal Dutch Shell, Exxon Mobil, Wal-Mart Stores, BP, Sinopec Group, China National Petroleum, State Grid, Chevron, ConocoPhillips, Toyota Motor, Total, Volkswagen, Japan Post Holdings, Glencore International, Gazprom, and E.ON (http://money.cnn.com/magazines/fortune/global500/2012/full_list/).

Table 3.14 Dynamics of the quantity of TNC in selected countries

No.	Country	1990	1995	2000	2005	2010	2012
1	USA	715	512	1140	948	885	806
2	UK	381	338	668	482	491	531
3	Canada	93	172	385	252	349	374
4	Australia	76	126	200	180	309	312
5	Germany	139	450	322	374	186	286
6	Russia	1	34	62	66	357	201
7	France	116	240	346	222	152	192
8	Brazil	2	28	159	37	114	192
9	Spain	72	66	182	81	151	175
10	Sweden	31	79	164	115	112	135
11	India	3	32	80	94	115	127
12	China	–	45	92	217	155	120
13	Netherlands	69	68	174	126	105	119
14	Norway	12	34	112	78	89	97
15	Switzerland	28	66	168	67	53	79
16	Singapore	16	31	52	96	74	78
17	Denmark	19	36	86	90	87	69
18	Indonesia	3	12	26	30	62	69
19	Italy	71	126	142	118	112	66
20	South Korea	1	10	51	25	46	65
21	Japan	–	11	78	44	99	64
22	Ireland	11	43	70	42	37	61
23	Turkey	4	3	17	29	46	59
24	Belgium	27	46	103	64	80	56
25	Finland	14	75	85	53	38	50
Other		168	721	1316	1074	1180	1017
The world		2072	3404	6280	5004	5484	5400

Note: compiled by the authors on the basis of the sources (www.unctad.org/fdistatistics)

It is known that TNCs account for most global industrial production and investments in the economy. They have a significant influence on the scientific and technical progress in these countries by means of financing most research and development; they also stimulate modernization of existing and development of new competitive products, implement the newest technologies, increase tax revenues, and reduce unemployment. Besides all this, the formation of reproduction chains by TNCs leads to the deepening of the international division of labour: up to one-third of the total volume of global trade is accounted for by TNCs.

Thus, to conclude, it is possible to state that participation of a country in foreign trade operations has a major influence on the development of its economy. Owing to involvement in global trade, the state receives many benefits. However, it should be understood that "skimming the cream" is possible only when the economy is ready for foreign economic liberalization: it should have sustainable growth rates,

3.2 Role of Foreign Trade in the Development of National Economies in the...   45

develop competitive spheres of industrial production, and have high human potential. On the other hand, opening the internal market may lead to a range of economic, technological, and social problems which can be solved only by turning back to protectionism, which—under the modern conditions in which international economic relations are being developed—is very difficult.

The economy should be constantly and gradually prepared for the inevitable influence of foreign factors of development, primarily by strengthening the foreign trade component. Each year, the volume of global trade becomes more substantial,[6] and whether the country takes its place in global markets depends on its further development: as a raw material appendage of the more developed countries or as a full member engaged in international economic relations.

It should be noted that today a huge role for the members of External economic relations (EER) belongs to the Eastern direction of foreign policy and FEA, as Asian countries show the highest indicators of growth of their economies, possess relative advantages expressed by the availability of a cheap workforce, and have free markets of goods and services. In particular, according to the estimates for the development of trade relations by HSBC, at the beginning of the twenty-first century the largest trade growth will be observed in Egypt, India, Indonesia, China, and Brazil. For example, by 2025—owing to the growth in production—the share of China in global trade will achieve 13.0 %, which will give it the leading position in the global economy (http://www.hsbc.ru/1/PA_1_1_S5/content/russia/about_us/news/pdf/rus/Press_release_Global_trade_forecast_from_HSBC_RUS_11_10_2011.pdf).

The countries which have not yet entered active foreign economic relations or have faced economic problems because of unwisely built models for foreign trade relations should correct their foreign trade policy in view of existing comparative advantages, the possibility of creation and growth of competitive advantages, and, of course, the optimal—from the point of view of transaction costs—vector of the country.

---

[6]In the following five years, the volumes of the global trade will be growing annually by 4.0 %, and in 2017–2021—by approximately 6.0 % [226].

Chapter 4
Role and Meaning of Foreign Trade Cooperation in the Globalizing World Through the Example of Russia and China

Abstract This chapter is devoted to an evaluation of the Russian economy's readiness for the development of foreign trade cooperation and substantiating the necessity for it between Russia and China. The authors study the dynamics of change in the sectorial structure of the Russian economy and a range of partner countries for international organizations, view the commodity structure for exports and imports in Russia, observe the level of openness in the Russian economy, determine the share of certain countries in Russian foreign trade turnover, and study the dynamics of the main indicators of Russian foreign trade, the dynamics of Russia's international reserves, and the demographics of organizations' ownership forms.

The authors conduct a SWOT analysis of the Russian economy in modern conditions and a general analysis of foreign trade turnover in Russia, determining the leading commodity group in the country's exports and imports. This chapter also views Russian foreign trade with its main trading partners, observes the comparative characteristics of Russian commodity turnover with the Commonwealth of Independent States (CIS) and non-CIS countries for the leading commodity groups, performs an analysis of the situation in the external sphere, and examines Russian national interests and priorities, the level of development of foreign economic institutes, and the country's position in the national economy in the context of the "Turn to the East" strategy. The authors prove the necessity for activation of cooperation with developing Asian countries—primarily with China.

4.1 Evaluation of Readiness of Russia's Economy for Development of Foreign Trade Cooperation

Today, Russia, as a member of international society, conducts a foreign economic policy which corresponds both to the achieved level of the country's internal economic development and to the requirements of the international structures of which it is a member.

Over a long period, its advantages have been a good geo-political location, rich raw materials, and relatively cheap energy, on the basis of which the sectorial structure of the economy is built.

Modern Russia, like all other countries of the Commonwealth of Independent States (CIS) and BRICS (Brazil, Russia, India, China, and South Africa), is a purely industrial country, though movement towards post-industrialization, in which most success has been achieved by the G7 countries (USA, Canada, Great Britain, Germany, Italy, France, and Japan), is clear (Table 4.1):

1. The share of industrial production in Russia's GDP has reduced from 48.4 % in 1990 to 36.3 % in 2013. Among the CIS countries, over 1990–2013, the share of this sphere grew only in Azerbaijan (maximum value among the counties of this group—66.8 % in 2011). The smallest share is observed in Moldova—16.6 %. Within the BRICS, the largest share of the corresponding sphere is observed in China—43.9 %, the minimum in Brazil—25.0 % in 2013. Among the countries in this group, the value of these indicators for all members does not exceed 30.0 %.
2. The share of agriculture in Russia's GDP reduced abruptly from 16.6 to 3.9 % in 1990–2013. It is the smallest indicator among the CIS countries (maximum is 27.4 % in Tajikistan). Among the BRICS countries, only South Africa had a share smaller than Russia's (2.3 %) in 2013. In the G7 countries, agriculture does not exceed 2.3 %.
3. The share of services in Russia's GDP prevails. In 1990–2013, it grew from 35.0 to 59.8 %. Among the CIS countries, the figure is largest in Moldova (68.4 %). Among the BRICS countries, in 2013 Russia was exceeded in the value of the service sphere by Brazil (69.3 %) and South Africa (67.8 %). Great Britain is the leader in the G7 regarding services—79.1 %.

Despite the prevailing character of its service sphere, Russia's standard and quality of living depend on the effectiveness of industrial production's development, as industrial product dominate the country's exports (Table 4.2). The revenue share of Russia's federal budget as of year-end 2014 included customs charges (32.0 %) and minerals extraction tax (19.7 %) (http://www.economy.gov.ru).

This situation suggests a range of questions. If the share of industrial production in GDP is tending to reduce, and its products still determine the country's specialization in the international division of labour, what is the future of Russia in terms of foreign trade policy? Should the country "narrow" its industrial production just to the export of raw materials, which are currently in high demand, and then concentrate on development of the service sphere? Should the country try to preserve the existing volume of industrial production by diversification, and start to search for new niches in global markets and for new foreign trade partners?

It is obvious that these questions can only be answered after studying Russia's sectorial policy and its foreign economic policy. It seems that the most convenient tool is SWOT analysis (strengths, weaknesses, opportunities, and threats) of the Russian economy under modern conditions.

4.1 Evaluation of Readiness of Russia's Economy for Development of...

Table 4.1 Dynamics of changes of sectorial structure of the economy of Russia and certain countries–partners in international organizations, %

Country	1970			1980			1990			2000			2010			2013		
	Industry	Agriculture	Services	Industry	Agriculture	Services	Industry	Agriculture	Services	Industry	Agriculture	Services	Industry	Agriculture	Services	Industry	Agriculture	Services
Countries of the CIS																		
Russia	–	–	–	–	–	–	48.4	16.6	35.0	37.9	6.4	55.6	34.7	3.9	61.4	36.3	3.9	59.8
Armenia	–	–	–	–	–	–	52.0	17.4	30.7	39.0	25.5	35.5	37.0	19.2	43.8	31.5	21.9	46.6
Azerbaijan	–	–	–	–	–	–	32.9	29.0	38.1	45.3	17.1	37.5	64.1	5.9	30.0	62.1	5.7	32.2
Belarus	–	–	–	–	–	–	47.1	23.5	29.4	39.2	14.2	46.7	42.2	10.6	47.2	42.2	9.1	48.7
Kazakhstan	–	–	–	–	–	–	–	–	–	40.5	8.7	50.8	42.9	4.8	52.3	36.9	4.9	58.2
Kyrgyzstan	–	–	–	–	–	–	35.0	33.5	31.4	31.4	36.7	51.4	29.2	19.4	51.4	26.7	17.7	55.6
Moldova	–	–	–	–	–	–	36.7	36.1	27.2	21.7	29.0	49.2	15.9	14.4	69.7	16.6	15.0	68.4
Tajikistan	–	–	–	–	–	–	37.6	33.3	29.1	38.9	27.4	33.7	28.2	22.1	49.7	21.7	27.4	50.9
Turkmenistan	–	–	–	–	–	–	29.6	32.2	38.2	44.4	24.4	31.2	48.4	14.5	37.1	–	–	–
Uzbekistan	–	–	–	–	–	–	33.0	32.8	34.3	23.1	34.4	42.5	32.5	19.1	48.4	26.3	19.1	54.6
Ukraine	–	–	–	–	–	–	44.6	25.6	29.9	36.3	17.1	46.6	31.3	8.3	60.4	26.9	10.4	62.7
Countries of the BRICS																		
Brazil	38.3	12.3	49.4	43.8	11.0	45.2	38.7	8.1	53.2	27.7	5.6	66.7	28.1	5.3	66.6	25.0	5.7	69.3
India	20.5	42.0	37.6	24.3	35.4	40.3	26.5	29.0	44.5	26.0	23.0	51.0	27.2	18.2	54.6	30.7	18.0	51.3
China	40.5	35.2	24.3	48.2	30.2	21.6	41.3	27.1	31.5	45.9	15.1	39.0	46.7	10.1	43.2	43.9	10.0	46.1
South Africa	38.2	7.2	54.7	48.4	6.2	45.4	40.1	4.6	55.3	31.9	3.3	64.8	30.2	2.6	67.2	29.9	2.3	67.8
Countries of the G7																		
USA	35.2	3.5	61.2	33.5	2.9	63.6	27.9	2.1	70.1	23.2	1.2	75.6	20.4	1.2	78.4	(2012) 21.0	(2012) 1.3	(2012) 77.7
Canada	35.1	4.7	60.2	36.9	4.3	58.8	31.3	2.9	65.8	33.3	2.3	64.5	27.7	1.5	70.8	–	–	–
Great Britain	42.1	2.9	55.0	40.7	2.1	57.2	33.8	1.8	64.4	26.9	0.9	72.2	20.6	0.7	78.7	20.2	0.7	79.1
Germany	48.1	3.7	48.2	41.1	2.4	56.5	37.3	1.5	61.2	30.8	1.1	68.1	30.0	0.7	69.3	30.7	0.9	68.4
Italy	39.3	8.8	52.0	38.1	6.0	55.9	32.0	3.5	64.5	27.1	2.8	70.1	24.4	2.0	73.6	23.3	2.3	74.4
France	35.1	8.1	56.8	31.3	4.9	63.3	27.1	4.2	68.7	23.3	2.3	74.4	19.6	1.8	78.6	19.8	1.7	78.5
Japan	43.5	5.1	51.3	39.0	3.1	57.9	37.5	2.1	60.4	31.1	1.6	67.3	27.5	1.2	71.3	(2012) 25.6	(2012) 1.2	(2012) 73.2

Note: compiled by the authors on the basis of the sources (http://www.worldbnk.org)

Table 4.2 Commodity structure of export and import of Russia (in %)

Commodity group	1995 Export	1995 Import	2000 Export	2000 Import	2005 Export	2005 Import	2010 Export	2010 Import	2014 Export	2014 Import
Mineral commodities	42.5	6.4	53.8	6.3	64.8	3.1	69.9	2.3	70.5	2.5
Metals, precious stones, and items made of them	26.7	8.5	21.7	8.3	16.8	7.7	12.9	7.3	10.5	7.1
Products of chemical industry, gum elastic	10.0	10.9	7.2	18.0	6.0	16.5	6.1	16.5	5.9	16.2
Machines, equipment, and transport means	10.2	33.6	8.8	31.4	5.6	44.0	5.2	45.4	5.3	47.6
Food products and agricultural raw materials (excluding textiles)	1.8	28.1	1.6	21.8	1.9	17.7	2.2	15.5	3.8	13.9
Timber and cellulose and paper items	5.6	2.4	4.3	3.8	3.4	3.3	2.5	2.6	2.3	2.1
Textiles, textile items, and footwear	1.5	5.7	0.8	5.9	0.4	3.7	0.1	6.1	0.2	5.7
Raw hide, furs, and items made of them	0.4	0.3	0.3	0.4	0.1	0.3	0.1	0.6	0.1	0.4
Other commodities	1.3	4.1	1.5	4.1	1.0	3.7	1.0	3.7	1.4	4.4
Total	100.0	100.0	100.0	100.0	100.0	100.0	100.0	100.0	100.0	100.0

Note: compiled by the authors on the basis of the sources (http://www.gks.ru)

We consider that the economy's strengths include, first of all, a rich raw material base. This has ensured the development of a range of extracting and processing industries. A second strength is the developed transport network of the country, represented by railway and motor transport, major pipelines, and navigable rivers.

Owing to a large territory and the climatic conditions, the main volume of freight operation is undertaken by railways and pipelines, which constitute 42.3 % and 51.0 % respectively of the freight turnover of the country (http://annrep.rzd.ru/reports/public/ru?STRUCTURE_ID=4389&). This transport infrastructure is constantly expanding. Currently, an investment project is aiming to create the Power of Siberia gas pipeline, and modernization of the main railway lines within the Eurasian Land Bridge project is being planned.

The weaknesses of Russia's economy include a low level of competitiveness in a range of processing industries, caused by non-conformity to present-day technologies, a lack of highly qualified specialists, the low quality of infrastructural development, and minimal investment.

These spheres include:

1. Domestic car industry (AvtoVAZ OJSC, KAMAZ OJSC, GAZ Group OJSC, Sollers OJAC, ZIL OJSC, BAZ OJSC, etc.). A common negative situation deepened after the 2000s when Russian car market was opened to foreign manufacturers. As a result, BMW, Chevrolet, Ford, Renault, Skoda, Toyota, and Volkswagen, and car alliances Kia, Nissan, Opel, Peugeot-Citroen-Mitsubishi, and Volvo Truck entered Russia. It may be taken as a given that that they will be unenthusiastic about the possibility of reviving the domestic car industry.

In our opinion, another advantage of the Russian economy is the high-quality scientific and technological bases for the manufacture of military products and dual-purpose products (which appeared in Soviet times) and the machine-building capabilities of the country.[1]

---

[1] In particular, Russia accounts for 27 % of the global weapons market, giving way only to the USA which accounts for 29 % (http://www.sipri.org/databases). Russia cooperates with more than 80 countries, supplying military products into 62 countries, including India, Venezuela, China, Vietnam, Algeria, Kuwait, Greece, Iran, and Brazil. The key enterprises in this sphere are the Izhevsk and Nizhegorodskiy machine building plants, and the Votkinskiy plant.

In 2001–2010, the total volume of foreign sales of Rosoboronexport OJSC grew by ten times, reaching $8.7 billion and constituting $13.2 billion in 2014 (http://www.ria.ru). A large share of Russian exports belongs to warplanes and dual-purpose products. As to the volume of the warplanes and war helicopters industry, Russia was ranked first in the world in 2014: 124 warplanes and 300 war helicopters were built in the country in 2014 (http://www.regnum.ru/news/polit/1898196.html#ixzz3SfMpVAn0).

In the sphere of civil aircraft engineering, Russia cooperates with almost all world manufacturers (Boeing, Airbus, Snecma, Embraer, etc.).

As for the rocket and space industry, its modern structure is represented by Roskosmos state corporation, which includes 50 enterprises, the largest of which are Korolev Rocket and Space Corporation Energia, Khrunichev State Research and Production Space Centre, Progress State Research and Production Rocket Space Centre, and the Lavochkin Research and Production

2. The sphere of micro-electronics and nano-technological production (Rosnano OJSC, Angstrem OJSC, NIIME and Micron OJSC, SITRONIX-Nano OJSC), which accounts for just 1 % of the global market.
3. Agriculture and food industry, in which Russia depends on the import of food products and agricultural machinery (up to 80 %). Russia has 10 % of all the arable land in the world, and development of agriculture has not been intensive but extensive in character, and a significant volume of food products is imported (13.9 % of the volume of imports in 2014). Agricultural exports (3.8 % of the volume of exports in 2014) of Russia is represented by grain—as of year-end 2014, Russia was ranked sixth in the world regarding the volume of export of grain (after the USA, India, France, Canada, and Australia), and third in the world for the volume of export of wheat (after the USA and Canada) (http://www.customs.ru). Today, agriculture is profitable and competitive (as of year-end 2014, profitability of agricultural manufacturers was 7.3 %, and the share of profitable agricultural organizations was 84.1 % (http://www.mcx.ru)), but there is a threat from foreign manufacturers. A reduction in state support for the agrarian sector, caused by Russia's entering the World Trade Organization (WTO) and changing domestic prices for production may lead to negative consequences for Russian agriculture and threaten national food security (http://expert.ru/south/2014/17/myi-mogli-poteryat-agrariev/?n=171).
4. Light industry, the share of which in the total volume of Russia's production is less than 1 %.

It is a pity that the service sphere does not have significant competitive advantages. This is true for telecommunications, finance, tourism, construction, the social sphere, and so on.

In particular, regarding the development of information technologies, Russia is not even among the top 20 countries of the world. According to the Networked Readiness Index, which is considered to be one of the most important indicators of a country's potential development, Russia was ranked 41st among 144 countries in 2014 (http://gtmarket.ru/ratings/networked-readiness-index/networked-readiness-index-info). According to the Index of Development of Information and Communication Technologies (2014), Russia is ranked 42nd (http://gtmarket.ru/ratings/ict-development-index/ict-development-index-info). In Internet development (2014) it

---

Association. Currently, Roskosmos has intergovernmental contracts with more than 30 countries (USA, Sweden, India, Brazil, Argentina, Japan, and countries of the European Space Agency) (http://www.federalspace.ru/114).

In the sphere of machine-building, it is necessary to mention the strong positions of Russian manufacturers of agricultural machinery (Rostselmash, Chelyabinsk Tractor Plant LLC, Cheboksary Aggregate Plant OJSC), railway machine building (Transmasholding CJSC, Tikhvin Industrial Site JSC, Uralvagonzavod OJSC, Mordovia Carriage-Building Company OJSC, Vagonmash CJSC, Kaliningrad Carriage-Building Plant OJSC, Torzhok Carriage-Building Plant OJSC). A range of Russian carriage-building enterprises actively cooperate with foreign companies, among which are Alstom Group, American Railcar Industries Ltd, Amsted Rail, Nippon Sharyo Ltd, Siemens AG, and Starfire Engineering and Technologies.

is 55th (http://gtmarket.ru/ratings/internet-development/info). In E-government (2014) it is 27th (http://gtmarket.ru/ratings/e-government-survey/info). In IT (information technology) competitiveness (2014) it is 40th (http://gtmarket.ru/news/2014/05/29/6788).

Such a low level is caused by a range of factors: an unsatisfactory environment for the conduct of business, the low quality of IT infrastructure, insufficiently qualified personnel potential, low development of research and development (R&D), and non-conformity of the market to the legal environment.

In its turn, the development of the country's financial sphere could be assessed by the ranking of credit solvency, the presence of transnational banks, volumes of investments, and so on.

As to the first indicator, as of year-end 2013, Russia—together with Brazil, Spain, and Mexico—enters the group iBBB+, giving way to the groups of countries with the rankings of iAAA (Switzerland and Norway), iAA+ (USA, France, Germany, Australia, and South Korea), iAA (Japan, Sweden, Netherlands, Great Britain, Austria, and Canada), iAA– (Luxembourg and Denmark), iA+ (China, New Zealand, and Israel), iA (Czech Republic, Finland, Belgium, and Saudi Arabia), and iA– (Italy and Slovakia) (http://www.ra-national.ru/?page=raiting-credit).

As for the development of banking, Russia is not among the global financial centres and does not have its own large transnational banks.

As to volumes of investments, Russia is not among the leaders either. Thus, according to the ranking of the most investment-attractive countries and the largest countries–investors, published by the *World Economic Journal*, Russia was ranked eighth in 2012 with a volume of direct foreign investments (DFI) of $51.4 billion. DFI per capita constituted $362.3. For comparison, the USA was ranked first with the corresponding indicators being $167.3 billion and $533.5, Hong Kong was third ($74.6 billion and $10,397.9), and Singapore was seventh ($56.7 billion and $10,481.2) (http://world-economic.com/ru/articles_wej-350.html).

Regarding Russia's direct investments, the picture is even more pessimistic—their negative growth may be observed, the greater part of them being transferred abroad (Table 4.3).

Domestic investors are primarily interested in the development of financial activities and insurance, wholesale and retail, production, and minerals extraction. The only positive aspect is that among the attracted domestic direct investments a significant part accounts for R&D.

Table 4.3 Dynamics of direct investments of Russia ($ million)

Indicator	2000	2005	2010	2011	2012	2013	2014
Direct investments, including	−501	−2372	−9448	−11,767	1766	−17,288	−33,502
– Abroad	−3179	−17,880	−52,616	−66,851	−48,822	−86,507	−56,393
– Into Russia	2678	15,508	43,168	55,084	50,588	69,219	20,891

Note: compiled by the authors on the basis of the sources (http://www.cbr.ru)

Portfolio investments into Russia constitute 1 % of the total inflow of foreign investments (http://www.gks.ru). Foreign investments are interested primarily in securities in the largest Russian companies: Gazprom OJSC, NC Rosneft OJSC, NC Lukoil OJSC, TNC-VR Holding OJSC, Sberbank of Russia OJSC, Surgutneftegaz OJSC, Novatek OJSC, Norilskiy Nikel, and RUSAL, for example.

The Russian tourist industry has a large potential but relatively low indicators of development. On the one hand, the country has a lot of resorts: resorts that exploit the Caucasus mineral waters (Essentuki, Zheleznovodsk, Kislovodsk, Kumagorsk, Nagutsk, and Pyatigorsk), the Black Sea coast of the Caucasus (Sochi, etc.), Moscow, St Petersburg, the Golden Ring cities, Lake Baikal, and so on. On the other hand, as of year-end 2014, Russia was ranked 45th for its level of competitiveness in travel and tourism (http://gtmarket.ru/news/2015/05/07/7152); even so, Russia is among the top ten countries as regards the number of incoming tourists and profits from this area.

In the socially important spheres of education, science, and healthcare the situation is similar: the potential is high, but Russia's ranks in intercountry comparisons are medium.

In particular, as regards the level of education in the country, determined by UN experts, as of year-end 2014, Russia was ranked 49th.

As to the level of expenses for R&D in relative measurement, the 2012 top five was made up of Israel, Finland, South Korea, Sweden, and Japan. Russia was ranked 32nd. As to expenses for R&D per capita, Russia is not even among the top ten. According to the absolute calculation of expenses, Russia is ranked tenth.

As to one of the key indicators of the level of R&D activity, which is the number of R&D articles published in peer-reviewed scientific journals and included in the databases Science Citation Index (SCI) and Social Sciences Citation Index (SSCI), as of year-end 2014, Russia was ranked 15th.

According to the global index of innovations, calculated by the INSEAD business school methodology, Russia was ranked 49th as of year-end 2014.

In its turn, development of healthcare in the country also faces a range of problems: these include insufficient financing and the small number of domestic practical scientific developments. In particular, as to expenses in this sphere, calculated as a percentage of GDP, Russia was ranked 93rd as of year-end 2013 (http://gtmarket.ru/ratings/expenditure-on-health/info). According to data from the World Healthcare Organization, for 2000–2013 only India and China spent less on healthcare among the BRICS countries. A similar picture is observed with expenses calculated per capita. It should be noted that the volume of direct state expenses in Russia is higher than in other BRICS countries.

Nevertheless, the potential in this sphere is huge. Russia prepares a sufficient number of doctors who—with the proper level of material and technical support—could provide for the development of healthcare.[2]

---

[2]In particular, as to the share of doctors for 1,000 people, Russia is among the leaders with 4.309. In the USA this indicator is only 2.42; in France 3.381; in Italy 3.802; in Japan 2.14; and in China 1.456 (http://apps.who.int/gho/data/node.main.75?lang=en).

Moving on to the potential reserves that might allow for the growth of the country's economy, they include the following.

Firstly, the large internal market is not yet filled with the products of Russian manufacturers. The completion of investment projects that are aimed at manufacturing competitive products in the processing sector would allow the reduction of dependence on imported products and would allow the development of Russian foreign trade by means of the export of products that have a high share of added value.

Secondly, the orientation of foreign economic policy in a free-trading model allows domestic manufacturers not only to participate in the acquisition of foreign states' markets but also foreign companies—allowing them to be full subjects of the Russian economy. This is proved by the indicator of openness of the country's economy, which has grown as compared to the 1990s (Table 4.4), and a decreasing value of import taxes. In particular, it is expected that within the activities of the Customs Union (Russia, Belarus, and Kazakhstan) the average rate of import taxes will be reduced from 9.64 % in 2011 to 5.9 % in 2015; and by 2019, the average rate of custom tax in Russia is to constitute 5.0 % to 5.3 % owing to Russia's membership of the WTO (http://www.economy.gov.ru).

Thirdly, existing commodity niches in world markets guarantee—in the mid-term—the inflow of foreign currency into Russia's budget. Primarily, this inflow should be expected from the countries that are important partners in foreign trade operations (China, Netherlands, Germany, Italy, Turkey, and Japan) and from those countries with which an increase in commodity turnover is potentially possible (Belarus and Kazakhstan, as members of the Customs Union of the Eurasian Economic Community, EurAsEc) and new industrial countries: Hong Kong, Indonesia, Malaysia, Singapore, and Taiwan, which share in the commodity turnover as Russia grows (Table 4.5).

Fourthly, a positive trade balance of the country, which means an excess of all payments from trade that come into the country from abroad over the payment from Russia into other countries, and provides the growth of currency reserves of the country, guarantees the stock of reserves in the internal market for foreign products without damaging the interests of domestic manufacturers (Table 4.6).

Fifthly, a small (as compared to GDP) external debt of the country (which as of 1 January 2015 constituted $597.3 billion, or 29.0 % of its nominal GDP)

Table 4.4 Dynamics of the level of openness of Russia's economy in 1995–2014

Year	WTO $ billion	Export	Import	GDP (nominal values), $ billion	Level of openness of economy
1995	145.0	82.4	62.6	395.5	0.37
2000	149.9	105.0	44.9	259.7	0.58
2005	363.9	240.0	123.8	764.0	0.48
2010	638.4	392.7	245.7	1524.9	0.42
2013	864.6	523.3	341.3	2096.8	0.41
2014	805.8	497.8	308.0	1860.6	0.43

Note: compiled by the authors on the basis of the sources (http://www.cbr.ru)

Table 4.5 Share of certain countries of the world in foreign trade turnover of Russia, %

Country	1995	2000	2005	2010	2011	2012	2013	2014
China	3.4	4.5	6.0	9.5	10.1	10.5	10.5	11.3
Netherlands	3.9	3.7	7.8	9.3	8.3	9.9	9.0	9.4
Germany	10.2	9.6	9.7	8.4	8.7	8.8	8.9	9.0
Italy	4.2	6.2	6.9	6.0	5.6	5.5	6.4	6.2
Belarus	4.1	6.8	4.7	4.5	4.8	4.3	4.1	4.0
Turkey	1.7	2.5	3.7	4.0	3.9	4.1	3.9	4.0
Japan	3.2	2.4	2.8	3.7	3.6	3.7	3.9	3.9
USA	5.6	5.4	3.2	3.7	3.8	3.4	3.3	3.7
Ukraine	11.0	6.3	5.9	5.9	6.2	5.4	4.7	3.6
South Korea	1.0	1.0	1.9	2.8	3.0	3.0	3.0	3.5
Poland	2.4	3.8	3.3	3.3	3.4	3.3	3.3	2.9
Kazakhstan	4.2	3.2	2.9	2.4	2.5	2.7	2.8	2.7
India	1.3	1.2	0.9	1.4	1.1	1.3	1.2	1.2
Singapore	0.6	0.4	0.2	0.4	0.3	0.2	0.3	0.8
Brazil	0.4	0.5	0.9	0.9	0.8	0.7	0.7	0.8
Taiwan	0.4	0.4	0.6	0.5	0.5	0.6	0.8	0.7
Vietnam	0.3	0.1	0.3	0.4	0.4	0.4	0.5	0.5
Malaysia	–	–	–	0.3	0.2	0.2	0.3	0.4
Indonesia	–	–	–	0.3	0.3	0.3	0.4	0.3
Hong Kong	0.3	0.1	0.1	0.1	0.1	0.2	0.4	0.2

Note: compiled by the authors on the basis of the sources (http://www.customs.ru)

Table 4.6 Dynamics of main indicators of Russia's foreign trade, $ million

Indicators	1995	2000	2005	2010	2014
Export	82,419	105,003	240,024	392,674	497.8
Import	62,603	44,862	123,839	245,680	308.0
Trade balance	19,816	60,172	116,185	149,995	189.8
Payment balance (current operations)	6969	46,839	84,389	67,452	56.7

Note: compiled by the authors on the basis of the sources (http://www.cbr.ru)

characterizes Russia as a relatively reliable partner that is able to fulfil its accumulated financial obligations before external creditors (http://www.cbr.ru).

Sixthly, the accumulated international reserves of Russia, with the Bank of Russia and the Government of Russia, might and should be used for elimination of the trade balance deficit, influencing the exchange rate of currency through currency operations, and supporting trust in the national currency (Table 4.7).

Over recent years, the gold and forex reserves of Russia have increased from $6.5 billion to $509.6 billion (1995–2014; the maximum was reached in August 2008, constituting $598.1 billion)—primarily, by means of a favourable foreign trade situation and growing volumes of exports. However, after the implementation of economic sanctions against Russia in early 2014, a reduction in oil prices, and Russia's Central Bank conducting measures to support the rouble and providing currency credits for banks, the volume of gold and forex reserves reduced to $358

Table 4.7 Dynamics of international reserves of Russia (as of 1 January) ($ billion)

Indicator	1995	2000	2005	2010	2011	2012	2013	2014	2015
International reserves (total), including	6.5	12.5	124.5	439.5	479.4	498.6	537.6	509.6	385.5
Currency reserves	4.0	8.5	120.8	416.7	443.6	454.0	486.6	469.6	339.4
Monetary gold	2.5	4.0	3.7	22.8	35.8	44.7	51.0	40.0	46.1

Note: compiled by the authors on the basis of the sources (http://www.cbr.ru)

billion as of August 2015. The similar reduction was observed during the global financial crisis—from $598.1 billion in August 2008 to $376.1 billion in March 2009 (http://www.cbr.ru).

In turn, the possible threats which come from the external environment, and might change the path of Russia's future development, include the following.

Firstly, there is the probability that Russia's status as a raw materials appendage of post-industrial and new industrial export-oriented countries will be established beyond doubt, which will actively develop industrial production. This picture could be aggravated as a result of a depletion of the country's resources base and the loss of a range of spheres in the Russian economy in which the level of competitiveness is currently very low.

Secondly, a loss of control over Russian business could be a consequence of the annual liquidation of a large number of domestic organizations and also the expansion of foreign property ownership in the Russian market.

In particular, growth in the number of registered organizations belonging to foreigners and a low rate of their liquidation may be observed (Table 4.8).

Thirdly, there is the growing dependence of Russia's internal economic development on the situation in the global commodity markets, whose products flood into the internal market of the country, satisfying demand from the population (consumer products) and also domestic manufacturers (components). This is proved by Russia's import quota—16.4 %.

Fourthly, the situation regarding labour resources in the internal market does not conform to the development of the state. Russia's population in 2014 constituted 146.2 million, of which the number of the employed was 71.5 million (48.9 %) with 3.8 million unemployed (5.2 % of economically active population). On the one hand, Russia faces the problem of an uncontrolled inflow of cheap labour resources, but on the other hand, a lot of highly qualified specialists leave Russia every year.

In particular, over 2003–2013, the largest migration growth in Russia took place as a result of arrival of citizens of Uzbekistan (446,500), Kazakhstan (331,000), Ukraine (303,400), Armenia (239,000), and Tajikistan (197,500). For comparison purposes, it should be noted that during the same period, people left Russia for Germany (93,100), USA (17,300), Finland (5100), Canada (4800), and Spain (2500) (http://www.gks.ru).

Emigration flows from Russia continue to follow the paths established back in the 1990s: Uzbekistan (85,900), Tajikistan (32,600), Ukraine (29,700), Armenia (20,600), and Kazakhstan (16,500). The traditional countries for emigration also include Germany, Israel, and the USA. However, it should be noted that outflow to

Table 4.8 Demography of organizations for property forms (January–November of the corresponding year)

Ownership form	Number of registered organizations				Number of officially liquidated organizations			
	2005		2014		2005		2014	
	Total	For 1000 organizations[a]	Total	For 1000 organizations	Total	For 1000 organizations	Total	For 1000 organizations
Total, including	394,514	89.7	402,589	85.5	83,033	18.9	380,001	80.7
Russian	384,557	89.5	392,833	85.8	81,996	19.1	369,873	80.8
Foreign	5404	113.4	6656	85.0	445	9.3	6587	84.1
Joint	4553	86.9	3100	60.9	592	11.3	3541	69.5

Note: compiled by the authors on the basis of the sources (http://www.gks.ru)
[a]Organizations accounted in the Statistics Register of the Federal State Statistics Service

these countries has decreased recently. For example, in 2014, 4442 people left for permanent residence in Germany, while in 2006–2013 the outflow constituted 8200–3900 annually, and in the previous years it was 20,000–40,000 annually. The volume of migration outflow to the USA reduced as well, from 4700 in 2000 to 1800 in 2014 (http://www.gks.ru).

Besides the traditional migration partners, a large role in the formation of the Russian labour market belongs to China. There is a tendency towards growth in the number of migrants from this country (9900 in 2014 against 5100 in 2011), with a corresponding reduction in the number of people leaving Russia for China.

Fourthly, finance is being transferred into offshore havens, uncontrolled by the state, leading to less investment in future development and losses in the Russian budget.

According to expert evaluations, in 2012 more than $111 billion worth of Russian products passed through offshore accounts—one-fifth of all Russian exports. Half of the $50 billion of Russian investments into other countries is also accounted for by offshores (http://www.президент.рф).

Thus, concluding this analysis of the state of Russia's economy and its potential reserves for growth, together with threats from the external environment, it is possible to state that the country possesses a gigantic potential for development, yet is turning into a monoculture partner in foreign trade operations and occupies "narrow" commodity niches in the global markets, specializing in the international division of labour only in resource-intensive (energy) production (Table 4.9). Unfortunately, the opinion that Russia is a uniquely wealthy but insufficiently competitive country is supported by international society, as is seen in the rankings from international economic organizations.

It should be understood that in view of the low competitiveness of a large number of spheres of the country's economy, growing accessibility of Russian production for foreign capital, and niches that are occupied in global commodity markets (most of which are defined by tough competition), the diversification of the sectorial policy of Russia should be built not so much on theoretical postulates about the significance of the knowledge factor in the development of economic subjects as on the wise choice of partners in foreign trade, focusing on areas where internal markets are growing and ready to purchase Russian products with a higher (as compared to today) level of processing.

It seems that in the current situation Russia should emphasize the changing of the sectorial structure of its economy and the optimization of its foreign trade policy.

Thus, based on Chap. 1, it is possible to draw the following conclusions.

Firstly, among all the possible services, which are objects of trade, trade occupies a specific place, as it performs a unique function of exchange. This is related to all its types and forms, as well as its method of conduct. Proper understanding of this function at state level allows the country and the commodity structure of export/import to change for the purpose of national development. Mutually profitable "exchange"—but not simple "sale"—has been viewed and is being viewed by the representatives of various schools and directions of economic thought within the theories of international trade.

Secondly, according to the economists and the data of real statistics, the importance of foreign trade for economic development of the state is huge. If the

Table 4.9 SWOT analysis of Russian economy under modern conditions

Pros	Cons
Rich resource base, represented by oil, natural gas, coal, uranium, diamonds, copper, ferrous metal ores, gold, silver, forest and hydro-resources, and arable lands	
1. Existing and competitive extracting industry which brings revenues into the country's budget	1. Exploitation of natural resources, resulting in their depletion and changes in structure of the economy
2. Processing spheres of industry which function on the basis of domestic raw materials sources (with created material and technical basis, reliable partners, and consumer network)	2. Weak involvement of the resources extracted in the country in the processes of creation of products with higher level of processing and growth level of internal economic development of the country
3. Conduct of modernization in the sphere of iron industry which increases the level of competitiveness of manufactured products	3. Low competitiveness of processing spheres of economy, based on domestic resource base: oil refining, chemical industry and pharmaceutical industry related to low level of processing of created products and leading to necessity for attraction of foreign investments for further development
4. Competitive sphere of non-ferrous metallurgy, based on own raw materials and cheap electric energy	4. Low level of elaboration of domestic timber, related to lack of corresponding material and technical base
5. Developed energy sector of the country, represented by thermal stations, hydro-electric power stations, and atomic power stations which volumes of production fully cover internal demand for corresponding products	5. Insignificant use of alternative sources of energy
	6. Extensive character of development of agriculture, which competitive advantage in the global market is related to pricing factors, not to technological base
Scientific and technological production base which remained from Soviet times	
6. Created material and technical basis of military–industrial complex, space and rocket industry, and machine building (technologies developed in twentieth century)	7. Reduction of the level of competitiveness of military–industrial complex and space and rocket industry owing to decrease of their scientific component
	8. The products manufactured by Russian car industry and light industry which do not conform to the modern level of scientific and technological development and demands of consumers
	9. Weak modernization of main areas of food industry
Achieved level and quality of development of the service sphere	
7. The developed transport network of the country with domination of railways and pipelines in the sphere	10. Insignificant role in development of the country's economy of water and car transport
	11. High tariffs for services provided by railway transport

(continued)

4.1 Evaluation of Readiness of Russia's Economy for Development of... 61

Table 4.9 (continued)

Pros	Cons
	12. Weak development of domestic sea transport
	13. Low investment attractiveness of the country in the sphere of portfolio investments
	14. Low—in relation to the leading countries—level of development of information technologies
	15. Role of tourism in the country's economy that does not conform to the existing potential
8. Existing banking infrastructure. Growing investment attractiveness of the country in the sphere of DFI	16. Low level of education, as compared to leading countries
	17. Financing of R&D is insufficient for effective development of economy. Low level of R&D activity and innovational development
	18. Low effectiveness of healthcare owing to insufficient financing and small number of domestic practical developments
Possibility of development	Threats from external environment
1. Large internal market of the country and creation of the EurAsEc Customs Union	1. Preservation of demand for Russian raw materials and products with low added value in the global markets, which increases the possibility of Russia's turning into raw material appendage of countries that are leaders of globalization and new industrial countries and depletion of the resource base
2. Policy of free trade which opens Russian borders for domestic and foreign manufacturers	2. Strengthening of competition from foreign manufacturers, which stimulates the loss of a range of spheres of Russian economy with low level of competitiveness
3. Existing commodity structure of export which guarantees revenues into the Russian budget in the mid-term	3. Expansion of the volumes of foreign property in the Russian market, which may lead to loss of control over business in the country as a result of liquidation of domestic organizations
4. Positive trade balance of the country that creates reserves for the growth of imports without harming the interests of domestic manufacturers	4. Dependence on the situation in the global markets of consumer products and components, used by domestic companies for manufacture of final products
5. Active payment balance of the country which stimulates growth of currency reserves	5. Poorly controlled international migration of labour resources, which creates imbalance in the Russian market of labour resources: uncontrolled immigration of cheap resources against the background of "brain drain"
6. Insignificant (as to the GDP) external debt which the country can pay	6. Transfer of financial assets into offshore havens, as a result of which the economy does not receive investment for its further development and the country's budget suffers losses

(continued)

Table 4.9 (continued)

Possibility of development	Threats from external environment
7. Growing international reserves of Russia which allow correcting currency and monetary policy of the country	8. Complex foreign political situation
	9. Instability of the national currency exchange rate
	10. Extension of sanctions and limitations against Russia

Note: compiled by the authors on the basis of the sources (http://www.cbr.ru)

country's economy is ready for foreign economic liberalization, it will demonstrate sustainable rates of growth, the competitive sphere of industrial production will develop, and human potential will improve. Wisely built foreign trade determines the volumes of products that are manufactured in the country (the domestic market can and should expand by means of opening niches in external markets); the volume of GDP and all macro-economic indicators of the system of national accounts; the share of received global income for expert operations and all further payments into budgets at various levels; and living standards in the country.

If the economy is not ready for participation in the processes of exchange of goods and services in the international markets, but its boundaries are opening, it may lead to the outflow of capital, a growth in dependence on exports, the ousting of domestic manufacturers from their own market, an increase in technological underrun from developed countries, de-industrialization in the production sector, and loss of competitiveness at almost all levels of analysis.

Thirdly, it was too early for Russia to enter the global environment, taking into account the model of foreign economic liberalization. Raw materials export, which had remained unchanged for decades, did not change as a result of reforms and even aggravated the imbalances in sectorial development: science-based services are developing very weakly against the background of the continued extraction of natural resources.

With significant reserves of growth and real possibilities for expansion in foreign trade, the country is turning into a monoculture partner in foreign trade operations, occupying a "narrow" commodity market in the global markets, specializing in the international division of labour only in resource-based (energy) products. This is caused by a low level of competitiveness in a large number of processing industries and in the service sphere, as well as in agriculture, and the huge dependence of the economy's development on external factors.

Fourthly, transitioning to the export of innovational products cannot be performed by Russia independently. It requires a strategic partner in foreign economic spheres, which, being interested in cooperation, can stimulate the increase in Russia's competitiveness and the competitiveness of its people.

4.2 Substantiation of the Necessity for Development of Cooperation Between Russia and China in Foreign Trade

The structure of foreign trade for Russia in its enlarged form is divided into countries of the EU, which, as of year-end 2014, accounted for 48.2 % of Russian commodity turnover, APEC (Asia-Pacific Economic Cooperation)—27.0 %, CIS—12.2 %, EurAsEC—7.1 %, and the Customs Union—6.7 % (http://www.customs.ru).

At present, the top ten leading foreign trade partners of Russia are China, the Netherlands, Germany, Italy, Belarus, Turkey, Japan, the USA, Ukraine, and Kazakhstan (Table 4.10). Among these countries, there has been an obvious strengthening of mutual interest in foreign trade over recent years: especially between Russia and Germany, Italy, and Kazakhstan. Beginning from the mid-2000s, the share of China in Russia's foreign trade operations has been constantly growing: in 2010, China exceeded Germany in the volume of commodity turnover with Russia for the first time, and still remains the leader when using this indicator.

Analysis of foreign trade turnover for the Russian Federation shows that the leading commodity group remains unchanged in exports and imports, but on the whole, the total commodity structure of the products that cross the Russian border varies when viewed by country (region) (Table 4.11).

Thus, a traditional Russian export is "products of fuel and energy complex" (FEC). In 2014, the share of these products as related to the total commodity structure of Russian exports into foreign countries was 74.1 %, and into CIS countries it was 45.5 %.

In Russian imports, the largest share belongs to "machines and equipment"—its share in the total structure of imports from non-CIS countries was 50.5 % at year-end 2014, and from the CIS countries it was 29.4 %. A second important Russian import from non-CIS countries is "products of chemical industry" (16.8 %), and from the CIS countries it is "metals and products of metals" (18.1 %).

Thus, we would like to emphasize that it is very difficult to make the correct choice regarding the preferable direction of Russia's future foreign trade cooperation, when observing only the existing commodity structure of its exports and imports. Hypothetically, it could be any direction.

On the other hand, it should be understood that the modern age is one of power and hegemony of the strongest and most competitive states. Never before was the overwhelming character of development of a country treated by economists like this: national economies previously always had an opportunity to use protectionist measures or to avoid tough anthropogenic influences. Nowadays, the situation has changed drastically. After making decisions on structural reforms of the economy and which model of foreign trade policy to choose, countries have to take into account the influence of external factors, and only after that internal factors. The market of a country is "opened" by international structures not necessarily when the economy is ready (very often, it happens when the country is not ready, and its

Table 4.10 Foreign trade of Russia for the main countries, $ billion

Country	Foreign trade turnover						Export						Import					
	1995	2000	2005	2010	2014		1995	2000	2005	2010	2014		1995	2000	2005	2010	2014	
China	4.2	6.2	20.3	59.4	88.4		3.4	5.2	13.0	20.3	37.5		0.9	0.9	7.3	39.0	50.9	
Netherlands	4.8	5.1	26.6	58.4	73.2		3.2	4.3	24.6	54.0	68.0		1.6	0.7	1.9	4.4	5.2	
Germany	12.7	13.1	33.0	51.8	70.1		6.2	9.2	19.7	25.1	37.1		6.5	3.9	13.3	26.7	33.0	
Italy	5.2	8.5	23.5	37.4	48.5		3.4	7.3	19.1	27.4	35.7		1.9	1.2	4.4	10.0	12.7	
Belarus	5.2	9.3	15.8	28.0	31.5		3.0	5.6	10.1	18.1	19.7		2.2	3.7	5.7	10.0	11.8	
Turkey	2.2	3.4	12.6	25.2	31.1		1.6	3.1	10.8	20.4	24.4		0.5	0.3	1.7	4.9	6.7	
Japan	3.9	3.3	9.6	23.1	30.8		3.2	2.8	3.7	12.8	19.9		0.8	0.6	5.8	10.3	10.9	
USA	7.0	7.3	10.9	23.6	29.2		4.3	4.6	6.3	12.4	10.7		2.6	2.7	4.6	11.1	18.5	
Ukraine	13.8	8.7	20.2	37.2	27.9		7.1	5.0	12.4	23.1	17.1		6.6	3.7	7.8	14.0	10.7	
Kazakhstan	5.2	4.4	9.8	15.3	21.1		2.6	2.2	6.5	10.8	13.9		2.7	2.2	3.2	4.5	7.2	

Note: compiled by the authors on the basis of the sources (http://www.customs.ru)

4.2 Substantiation of the Necessity for Development of Cooperation Between...

Table 4.11 Comparative characteristics of commodity turnover of Russia with the foreign countries and CIS for the leading commodity groups, %

Commodity group	Export				Import			
	Non-CIS countries		CIS countries		Non-CIS countries		CIS countries	
	2010	2014	2010	2014	2010	2014	2010	2014
Share of the region in export/import	90.3	87.2	9.7	12.8	90.8	88.8	9.2	11.2
Food and agricultural raw materials	1.8	3.2	5.8	8.0	15.3	13.4	17.3	17.3
Mineral products, including	71.5	74.1	54.4	45.5	1.0	0.9	15.9	15.9
– Fuel and energy	70.8	73.3	53.0	43.9	0.7	0.5	10.5	10.5
Products of chemical industry, gum elastic	5.8	5.1	8.9	11.1	17.3	16.8	8.7	8.7
Raw hide, fur, and products made of them	0.1	0.1	0.0	0.1	0.6	0.5	0.1	0.1
Timber and cellulose and paper products	2.3	2.1	4.0	4.1	2.5	1.9	3.7	3.7
Textiles, textile products, and footwear	0.1	0.1	0.4	1.2	6.3	5.8	4.5	4.5
Precious stones, metals, and products made of them	2.5	2.7	0.2	0.4	0.2	0.3	0.2	0.2
Metals and products of metals	10.8	7.9	9.0	10.3	6.0	5.7	18.1	18.1
Machines, equipment, and transport means	4.3	3.7	14.4	16.3	47.0	50.5	29.4	29.4
Other	0.8	1.2	2.8	3.0	3.8	4.3	2.3	2.3
Total	100.0	100.0	100.0	100.0	100.0	100.0	100.0	100.0

Note: compiled by the authors on the basis of the sources (http://www.customs.ru)

manufacturers have yet to create a competitive advantage). As a result, developing countries are left at the periphery of global development, where they are given the role of serving the global reproduction cycles that have already been formed, and as a result, previously being the subjects of economies, they turn into the objects of geo-economic wars.

The negative aspect of this situation is levelled when developing countries understand their a priori "dependent" position in the global markets. If a country makes a decision about cooperation with a more developed partner and, what is more important, it can interest the partner, it means that, in the best case scenario, it will export industrial products while importing high-tech goods and services. In the worst case, exports will include not even the final products but separate components and will be combined with the import of industrial capital-intensive products. Even if the trade balance is positive, this will not mean that foreign trade has performed a positive role in the development of the national economy. As a consequence, developing countries with economic potential, a high-quality resource base (which they want to control at present and in future), and a small reserve of competitive advantages try to preserve their national sovereignty and guarantee a high level of national economic security—for this purpose they develop foreign trade policy, paying much attention to players with similar characteristics. There are many examples of this: almost all existing integration associations were created and continue to be created because of these reasons.

Regarding Russia, it means that the CIS countries are those with which integration should be deepened and mutual trade should be increased, thus raising the level of national competitiveness and "organizing a strategic maneuver for breakthrough to the global income" (Jahfer and Inoue 2014).

However, it should be understood that Russia is the most developed and richest state among the CIS countries. It would be difficult to solve such important problems such as development of R&D and attraction of investment into specific spheres of the national economy within various integration groups.

The task is somewhat simplified if the factors of the level that is achieved and the qualitative content of foreign trade cooperation are supplemented by the development of partner states and the rates and level of their economic development.

At the moment, intercountry relations are characterized by democracy, where each state can theoretically contribute to the development of the global economy, based on its specialization in the processes of the international division of labour, for most global commodity markets are open and liberal.

Regarding Russia, this means that it can increase cooperation with Germany, the Netherlands, Italy, Japan, and other developed countries (or at least preserve it at the current level).

Nowadays, Russia receives "technological imports" and consumer goods from developed countries and has a chance to bring revenue into its budget by means of the export of raw materials.[3] However, the inconsistent policy of the Western powers regarding Russia and the implementation of sanctions complicates further interaction with them and, as a SWOT analysis of the state of the Russian economy shows, is a threat to its development.

In this case, Russia, based on the situation in the outside world, Russian interests and priorities, and the level of development of foreign economic institutes, as well as the state of the national economy—within the accomplishment of the "Turn to the East" strategy—should activate cooperation with developed Asian countries, first of all with China.

---

[3]Thus, for example, as of year-end 2013, Germany imported goods into Russia in three major areas: car industry (€8.1 billion), machine building (€7.6 billion), and chemical industry (€3.2 billion). The Netherlands exports to Russia the following: machine-building products (€3.2 billion), chemical products (€1.0 billion), and food products (€0.9 billion). In its turn, the commodity structure of Russian imports from Italy is presented by machines, equipment, and transport (42.2 % of the total volume of import), consumer goods (35.9 %), and chemical products (7.3 %). The USA traditionally supplies machines, equipment, and transport (63.0 %): aircraft, spacecraft and their components, passenger cars, and other equipment and spare parts; products of the chemical industry (10 %), and food products and agricultural raw materials (9 %). Imports from Japan are formed by passenger and commercial vehicles, their spare parts and components, machines and equipment, construction and medical equipment, electric generators, electronics, and so on, which constitute approximately 85.0 % of the total (http://russian.china.org.cn/; http://www.ved.gov.ru).

There are several reasons for this.

Firstly, we think that Asia gives Russia a chance to "win time" for structural changes in its economy. At present, Russia is not ready for a tough competitive struggle with developed countries which possess such production factors as capital and knowledge. Russia should not presume that its manufacturers will soon learn to manufacture high-quality products with a large share of value added and restructure the global markets of corresponding goods—which were established a long time ago—thus beginning to occupy certain niches in them. If the country wants to leave the export of raw materials behind, the "Western direction" is not the best choice (even in the mid-term): countries with a higher level of economic development won't buy analogues of their own products that are made in Russia, and might even cost more.

Secondly, the choice of China from among the Asian countries is because it is a reliable foreign trade partner of Russia (in first place for commodity turnover). Besides, the development of Russian–Chinese relations is characterized by a rather large number of touch points of strategic interests in economic, political, social, ecological, humanitarian, and other spheres of activities. The countries organize a dialogue with each other both at national and transnational levels in such structures as the Shanghai Cooperation Organization, BRICS, APEC, and the UN Security Council. Specialists consider that effective relations between Russia and China determine the current global order. This is why cooperation between these two countries is being closely scrutinised by all countries, and studying the history of their relationship, which has deep roots right back to the seventeenth century, is an important direction for research.

This means that it is necessary to develop the existing agreements about mutual supplies, but it is also necessary to reconsider the policy concerning the use of financial assets raised by the export of Russian resources and the policy of taking imports from China, and to explore possibilities for cooperation as the Russian economy diversifies.

In the long term, it is necessary to reduce the share of products that are imported from China—primarily in the "machines, equipment, and components" category and science intensive products, through the manufacture of import-substituting products on Russian soil.

It is possible that the rate of further cooperation regarding raw materials should be preserved in the future, but the Russian side should use the profits obtained not for further exploitation of its own resource base and not as a means of financing technological imports (including those from China), but for development of the full production cycle of competitive spheres, and the spheres that are connected to the resource base of the country, on Russian territory. In particular, despite the fact that there is a tendency for Russia's share of exports to China to increase (Russia is the largest supplier of mineral products to China), its share is still insufficiently high, constituting less than 2.0 % (Table 4.12).

Thirdly, it is necessary to develop further cooperation with China because China is a growing economy with a large internal market that is ranked second in the world for GDP. At present, China is ranked first in the world for the volume of

Table 4.12 Dynamics of share of certain countries of the world in exports and imports of China, %

	Export			Import	
Country	2010	2014	Country	2010	2014
Korea	8.9	9.7	USA	17.0	16.9
Japan	12.8	8.3	Hong Kong	15.9	15.5
USA	8.7	8.1	Japan	7.8	6.4
Taiwan	7.5	7.8	Korea	4.1	4.3
Germany	5.2	5.4	Germany	3.9	3.1
Australia	4.5	5.0	Netherlands	2.9	2.8
Malaysia	3.5	2.8	Vietnam	1.9	2.7
Brazil	2.4	2.6	Great Britain	2.4	2.4
South Africa	1.4	2.3	Russia	1.9	2.3
Russia	1.8	2.1	India	2.6	2.3
Thailand	2.3	2.0	Singapore	1.7	2.1
Singapore	1.9	1.6	Taiwan	2.0	2.0
France	1.1	1.4	Malaysia	1.4	2.0
Indonesia	1.8	1.3	Australia	1.6	1.7
Canada	1.2	1.3	Indonesia	1.6	1.7

Note compiled by the authors on the basis of the sources (http://www.customs.gov.cn)

export of its products and second for the volume of imports, so its role in the formation of the climate of global markets of key export and import products is colossal. The most important tasks for China are to provide growth of the national economy of up to 8.0 % per year and further foreign economic expansion. In view of the research which has been conducted, this may be set in context through an analysis of the peculiarities of foreign trade development in China.

At the time of writing, China has a major share in global exports. As of year-end 2014, this was 12.3 %, which is especially impressive when compared to Russia's share of 2.6 % (Table 4.13). For Russia, this means there are potential niches for the export of domestically produced products.

It is important to note that China's economy, based on the existing structure of foreign trade operations, is balanced in its combination of exports and imports (Table 4.14). In particular, any increase in imports into the country is created by the stimulation of internal consumption.

The largest share of China's exports belongs to machine-building products and professional equipment (in 2014 this sector was 44.9 %) and products of light industry (15.2 %). It should be noted that the value of exports of machine-building products by China is 2.2 times larger than total Russian exports and 3.2 times larger than the value of exporting Russia's hydrocarbon resources. As of year-end 2014, China exported cell phones for $117.3 billion (http://www.customs.gov.cn) (as a comparison, at year-end 2014, Russia exported oil for $153.9 billion and natural gas for $54.7 billion) (http://www.gks.ru).

The leading imported groups of Chinese products as of year-end 2014 included products of machine building and professional equipment (36.4 %) and raw materials required for various spheres of industry (34.7 %) (Table 4.15).

4.2 Substantiation of the Necessity for Development of Cooperation Between... 69

Table 4.13 Dynamics of the share of China and Russia in global GDP (PPP) and global export, %

Indicator	1990		1995		2000		2005		2010		2014	
	PRC	RF	PRC	RF	PRC	RF	PRC	RF	PRC	RF	PRC	RF
Share in global GDP	3.6	4.7	5.6	2.6	7.1	2.4	9.4	3.0	13.2	3.7	16.6	3.4
Share in global export	1.6	2.2	2.7	1.8	3.9	1.7	7.3	2.3	10.4	2.6	12.3	2.6

Note: compiled by the authors on the basis of the sources (http://www.worldbnk.org)

Table 4.14 Dynamics of export and import quotas of China and Russia

Year	GDP, $ billion		Export quota, %		Import quota, %	
	China	Russia	China	Russia	China	Russia
1995	1811.1	832.7	8.1	9.9	7.5	7.5
2000	2985.4	998.3	9.4	10.5	8.4	4.5
2005	5364.3	1696.7	15.6	14.4	13.3	7.4
2010	10,084.8	2812.4	15.7	14.2	13.8	8.8
2011	11,290.9	3015.4	16.8	17.3	15.4	10.7
2012	12,470.9	3373.0	12.7	15.7	11.2	9.9
2013	16,162.0	3623.0	13.7	14.3	12.1	9.5
2014	18,017.0	3745.0	13.0	13.3	10.9	8.2

Note: compiled by the authors on the basis of the sources (http://www.worldbnk.org)

Table 4.15 Large commodity groups of exports and imports of China

Commodity group	2010		2014	
	$ billion	Share, %	$ billion	Share, %
Commodity structure of export				
Products of machine building and professional equipment	932.8	59.1	1051.7	44.9
Products of light industry	308.1	19.5	356.0	15.2
Products of chemical industry	124.6	7.9	199.1	8.5
Other goods	212.5	13.5	735.5	31.4
Total	1578.0	100.0	2342.3	100.0
Commodity structure of import				
Products of machine building and professional equipment	649.6	46.6	713.2	36.4
Raw materials for industry spheres	544.7	39.0	679.9	34.7
Other products	200.7	14.4	566.3	28.9
Total	1395.0	100.0	1959.4	100.0

Note: compiled by the authors on the basis of the sources (http://www.customs.gov.cn)

It should be noted that a high share of machines, equipment, and electronics among China's imports could be explained by the establishment of branches of transnational corporations in China. The production and technological processes of these enterprises are based on imported components and investment goods, with export of products and components following. In 2010, the enterprises created with participation of DFI provided 55.0 % of China's exports and 53.0 % of imports. As of year-end 2014, the share of exports for joint enterprises constituted 47.3 %, and imports 44.9 %. The industrial production of enterprises with DFI in GDP has reached 20 %, despite the fact that only 3 % of the country's workforce is employed by them. Average labour efficiency at the DFI enterprises is nine times higher than at national enterprises. According to estimates, DFI enterprises in China provide around 40 % of the growth in GDP; that is, without the products of these enterprises, China's economic growth would decrease from 9 % to 5 % (http://gasforum.ru/obzory-i-issledovaniya/232).

Today, China performs trading and economic operations with more than 220 countries and has intergovernmental trade agreements and protocols with most of them. The country's leading foreign trade partners are the USA (12.9 % of China's foreign trade turnover), Hong Kong (8.7 %), Japan (7.3 %), South Korea (6.8 %), Taiwan (4.6 %), and Germany (4.1 %). Russia accounts for 2.2 % of China's foreign trade turnover (Table 4.16).

The leading partners for China's export include the EU, the USA, Hong Kong, ASEAN, Japan, Republic of Korea, and Taiwan, which import the products of two leading groups of Chinese exports (machines, equipment, and components; electronics and components). The total share of exports for these commodity groups into the above countries constitutes approximately 42.0 %. Such countries as Russia, Australia, Saudi Arabia, India, and Brazil account for less than 5.0 % of the total volume of export of corresponding products.

Table 4.16 Foreign trade turnover of China with selected countries

Country	2010		2014	
	$ billion	Share, %	$ billion	Share, %
USA	385.3	13.0	555.1	12.9
Hong Kong	230.3	7.7	376.0	8.7
Japan	297.8	10.0	312.4	7.3
South Korea	207.2	7.0	290.5	6.8
Taiwan	145.4	4.9	198.3	4.6
Germany	142.4	4.8	177.8	4.1
Australia	88.1	3.0	136.9	3.2
Malaysia	74.2	2.5	102.0	2.4
Russia	55.4	1.9	95.3	2.2
Brazil	62.5	2.1	86.7	2.0
India	61.8	2.1	70.6	1.6
Other countries	1222.6	41.1	1901.5	44.2
Total	2973.0	100.0	4303.0	100.0

Note: compiled by the authors on the basis of the sources (http://www.customs.gov.cn)

Chinese products of light industry are in high demand in the markets of Australia, the EU, South Korea, Russia, Saudi Arabia, the USA, and Japan; their total share constitutes more than 10 %. Chinese products of the chemical industry are in high demand in the markets of Brazil, India, and Taiwan.

China's import partners could be divided into a range of groups, on the basis of the commodity niche that they occupy in the economy of the country. The first group includes Japan, the EU, the USA, Republic of Korea, Taiwan, partly Hong Kong, and ASEAN, the products being directly related to production processes of transnational corporations. The second group includes exporters of raw materials: Russia, Saudi Arabia, Australia, partly India, Brazil, and ASEAN. The third group includes exporters whose products compete with Chinese products in China: India, ASEAN, and, probably, Brazil.

Another (the fourth) reason for cooperation between Russia and China is its current leading position for manufacture of most types of industrial products. In particular, the volume of industrial production in China, as of year-end 2010, constituted $1.92 trillion (USA $1.86 trillion), (Popkova et al. 2013b) and in 2013 the volume of industrial production in China reached $4 trillion (USA $3.5 trillion) (http://www.stats.gov.cn). At present, China's share in the volume of global production of added value in the processing industries constitutes 18.4 %—second position in the world after the USA (19.3 %) (Table 4.17). China is also ranked fifth among 142 countries in indicators of competitiveness of national industry after Germany, Japan, USA, and South Korea. Russia is ranked 32nd in this ranking (http://www.unido.org).

A very important fact in this context is that China has managed—as a result of accelerated economic growth—to leave behind exclusively assembly production in favour of creation of the full production cycle. While China's exports were previously dominated by products of mass and labour-consuming products with low

Table 4.17 Share of selected countries in the global production of added value of processing industry, %

Role	Country	2005	2010	2014
1	USA	22.59	19.44	19.30
2	China	9.97	14.99	18.41
3	Japan	12.29	12.01	10.89
4	Germany	7.47	7.03	6.93
5	South Korea	3.11	3.79	4.01
6	Italy	3.88	3.21	2.69
7	Great Britain	3.38	2.80	2.54
8	France	3.29	2.79	2.46
9	India	1.60	2.26	2.31
10	Mexico	1.94	1.79	1.81
11	Brazil	1.86	1.82	1.59
12	Canada	2.22	1.66	1.58
13	Spain	2.10	1.69	1.51
14	Russia	1.63	1.50	1.51
15	Turkey	1.12	1.20	1.30

Note: compiled by the authors on the basis of the sources (http://www.unido.org)

Table 4.18 Dynamics of change of the commodity structure of China's exports, %

Indicator	1995	2000	2005	2010	2013
Industrial products, including	84.0	88.2	91.9	93.6	94.0
– Iron and steel	3.5	1.8	2.5	2.5	2.5
– Chemical products, including	6.1	4.9	4.7	5.5	5.4
Pharmaceutical products	1.1	0.7	0.5	0.7	0.6
– Products of machine building, including	21.1	33.1	46.2	49.5	47.1
Office and telecommunication equipment, including	9.7	17.4	29.7	28.5	26.9
Computers and office equipment	3.2	7.5	14.5	13.1	10.1
Telecommunication equipment	5.6	7.8	12.5	11.4	11.4
Integral schemes and electronic components	0.9	2.2	2.7	4.0	5.3
– Transport means	2.8	3.9	4.0	6.1	5.0
– Textile	9.3	6.5	5.4	4.9	4.8
– Clothes	16.1	14.5	9.7	8.2	8.0
Products of agriculture, including	10.1	6.6	3.8	3.3	3.2
– Food products	8.3	5.5	3.2	2.8	2.7
Fuel and products of ore mining spheres, including	5.6	5.0	4.1	3.0	2.7
– Fuel	3.6	3.2	2.3	1.7	1.5
Other	0.3	0.2	0.2	0.1	0.1
Total	100.0	100.0	100.0	100.0	100.0

Note: compiled by the authors on the basis of the sources (http://www.wto.int)

added value, the country is now developing the export of capital-intensive products, and the share of these is growing (Table 4.18).

This commodity structure of foreign trade operations is being achieved by China in an evolutionary way. Historically, the main export items were silk, china, products of timber, bone, and metal. The demand for these products from Mongolia, Korea, Japan, and the countries of Southeast Asia and Europe was one of the factors in the increase in their production volumes. However, such factors as tax and custom limitations, as well as state interference with trade and a range of other limitations caused by the feudal society, hindered the development of foreign trade (Delgado et al. 2012).

In the 1950s–1960s, the commodity structure of China's exports underwent radical changes: the country began to supply mainly raw materials and products of initial processing to external markets. Beginning in 1986, textile products ousted oil as a major export product. From that time on, China progressed from the export of raw materials to the export of labour-intensive products. Beginning in 1995, the largest share in the country's exports belonged to machine-building and electronics products, showing a transition from the export of labour-intensive products to capital-intensive and science intensive ones. Beginning in 2004–2005, China has become a leader in telecommunication equipment and the export of high-tech products.

For Russia, these changes mean that it acquires a chance to join the mass production of goods with a high level of processing, on the basis of the comparative advantages of China and its own advantages—both of a comparative and competitive character. In other words, there is a real possibility of cooperation.

Table 4.19 Dynamics of shares of traditional and give-and-take export in the total volume of export of China (I: volume, $ billion, II: share, %)

Forms of export	2005		2010		2011		2012		2013	
	I	II	I	II	I	II	I	II	I	II
Usual	315	42.3	667	42.3	917	48.3	539	44.3	1087	49.2
Tolling	416	56.6	728	46.1	835	43.9	618	50.7	860	39.0

Note: compiled by the authors on the basis of the sources (http://russian.china.org.cn/; http://www.ved.gov.ru)

In particular, the largest share in China's exports still belongs to products manufactured on a give-and-take basis (tolling) (Table 4.19).

This means that a proportion of industrial enterprises in China have the function of performing a certain share of the production process for foreign companies.

Russia should probably use this situation and offer cooperation with the Chinese. Emphasis should be placed on the possibility of joint production of science intensive rather than capital intensive products—especially as China is interested in the growth of the manufacture of high-tech products. The Chinese side should be motivated by the fact that Russia has an accumulated experience of work and competitive advantages in the production of, for example, military and dual-purpose products, material and technical base, corresponding technologies in machine building, a large resource base, and so on.

It is important to carefully and wisely choose the spheres of the Russian economy which should be developed on a joint basis. We consider that these might include only two areas:

1. The spheres in which Russia's position is still strong (the main goal of cooperation will be attracting investment to R&D and expanding the possibilities of corresponding manufacturers at the global commodity markets) or are connected to the resource base of the country (the main goal being to preserve control over resources and to save precious time that would otherwise be required for the creation of the country's own technologies, increasing the depth of processing of Russian resources by implementing previously used competing technologies);
2. Crisis spheres of the national economy, the development of which does not have high priority (it might be necessary to give up the issue of placement of new joint production on Russian territory in order to receive access to competitive technologies, and to allow for the revival of these spheres in the long term).

The spheres of the Russian economy that demonstrate a low level of competitiveness but have high potential for development should be revived independently on the basis of income from the export of raw materials.

As a result of cooperation, it is possible for Russia to manufacture high-tech products which are in high demand and competitive in global markets. In this case, the Russian side may receive from its partner the investments required for further development and for competitive technologies, and, what is more important, it will have a real chance to organize joint production on its soil, using Russian staff and receiving an impulse towards the development of infrastructure.

Chapter 5
Perspectives of Acceleration of the Rates of Economic Growth of Russia in the Context of Foreign Trade Cooperation with China

Abstract This chapter determines the main directions for the modernization of the Russian economy in view of the Asian factor in developing foreign trade connections for the country, and offers measures of state regulation and support for the fulfilment of Russian economic interests in foreign trade cooperation with China. The authors view the key tendencies of the development of the global economy in the twenty-first century and the 2008 crisis, study the index of global competitiveness of the World Economic Forum and its main components for Russia and China, and determine a range of obvious problems for development of the Russian economy and an increase in the level of its national competitiveness.

The authors offer suggestions for the direction that Russian foreign trade could take, including the development of cluster policy according to the "Concept of long-term socio-economic development of the Russian Federation until 2020" and the "Strategy of innovational development of the Russian Federation until 2020". The authors determine potential threats that may arise owing to increasing cooperation with China and develop measures of state regulation and support for the accomplishment of Russian economic interests as foreign trade cooperation with China increases.

5.1 Main Directions of the Modernization of the Russian Economy in View of the "Asian" Factor of the Country's Developing Foreign Trade Connections

The key development tendencies of the global economy during the twenty-first century, especially their manifestations after the 2008 crisis, showed that the future of the Russian economy, its effectiveness, profitability, competitiveness, and, most important, the possibility for preserving national sovereignty and national security, depend on wise foreign economic policy as a whole and the foreign trade component in particular.

Today, it is impossible to develop effectively while sticking to the policy of protectionism—because of internationalization and globalization processes, as well as institutional transformations which are taking place at the macro-level; that is, external factors, limitations in a country's resources, and, accordingly, reserves of growth, in other words internal factors. In the modern world, the key role in the global economy belongs to the players (sovereign states) that can build their foreign economic strategy taking into account their own comparative and competitive advantages and the similar advantages of key partner countries. In the globalized world, resources (intellectual, labour, financial, production, raw materials, energy, etc.) become international, and their national (territorial) context is in the background. Economic agents from various countries receive free and coordinated access to these resources for the purpose of maximizing global income.

The analysis that was conducted showed that in view of the transformations which take place in the global economy the main vector of foreign economic (and, accordingly, foreign trade) development for Russia should be Asia, primarily China. Russia has to correct its foreign economic policy, using any available resources—primarily, its own and Chinese (in other words, regardless of geographic location)—in order to realize the country's national purposes: preserving Russia as a sovereign entity with a high level of national competitiveness and maximizing received income from the export of products with a high share of added value.

On the whole, this task is not new. This necessity has been discussed for a long time, and there have been many meetings, conferences, and symposiums on the topic—even on a two-country basis.[1] However, foreign trade between the two countries—primarily, Russia—being in the "current of full liberalization", is performed without consideration of a possibility for an "Asian" vector of development.

Modern Russia is a powerful and energetic state (the analysis in Chap. 2 proved that). It possesses stocks of oil, natural gas, coal, uranium, diamonds, copper, ferrous metal ores, silver, timber, and so on, and is ranked in the top ten countries for the volume of known reserves and the volume of extraction. However, the main problem, in our opinion, is that the country's resource base is used extensively,[2] and unwisely: preserving it extending its use for our own purposes, or offering resources to foreign partners, not the final export products but the very deposits, is not seen as important. In other words, we build our foreign trade only on the theory of comparative advantages (forgetting about the conclusions drawn by merchants in the sixteenth century—which were discussed in Chap. 1). A country that hopes to take up a position as one of the global economic leaders and important players in the

---

[1] In particular, in September 2009, Shanghai, China hosted a round table "transformation processes of geo-economic space: Russia and China in multipolar world", devoted to the 60th anniversary of the establishment of diplomatic relations between Russia and China (http://www.rg.ru/2011/06/10/china.html).

[2] According to data from the UN International Trade Center, Russia holds the ten first positions (oil, natural gas, gas, aluminium, steel, nickel, timber, coal, etc.), making up 67.4 %, and the first three positions (oil, natural gas, and petrol)—53.8 % of the total Russian exports (http://www.intracen.org/tradstat/welcome.htm).

modern global order in the twenty-first century cannot only rely on its raw materials. Meanwhile, modern Russia preserves raw materials (more than 90%) in the commodity structure of national exports, but this makes up only 70% of the total cost of export for mineral products. The share of machine-building and professional equipment products accounts for only 5.0%.

Obviously, with such a structure for the country's exports, its main foreign trade partners are the countries that have a demand for raw materials, regardless of their economic, scientific, and technical development.

In its turn, China has a leading position in the global commodity markets in the twenty-first century with a wide assortment of complex products with a high share of added value. Accordingly, it is interested in the partners that can support it (both by investments and sales of their own technologies and by joint scientific research or sales of human and intellectual capital) as it further strives for the development of its own science intensive production. Under these conditions, the interests of the two countries are not equal: Russia is much more interested in China than China is in Russia.

We consider that when building its strategic plans for economic development, Russia should be basing them not only on its own comparative and competitive advantages but on the strong aspects of partner countries, taking into account its interests.

In particular, at the moment, according to the specialists from the Center of Strategic Vision (which is one of the departments of the World Economic Forum (WEF) that compiles an annual index of the global competitiveness of countries), the following indicators have positive dynamics for the development of the Russian economy (Fig. 5.1).

1. Development of institutes. For example, in the period 2012–2014, Russia went up in the rankings of the work of government institutes (from 133rd to 102nd position) and private institutes (from 125th to 88th position). This growth was caused by improvement in all intermediary indicators which characterize the situation in the country: ownership rights and protection of intellectual property, outflow of state assets, public mistrust of politicians, state of payments and bribes, wastage of state expenses, independence of judges, effectiveness of the legal system in the regulation of arguments, organized crime, reliability of police work, corporate ethics, quality of audits and accounting in private institutes, and protection of the interests of minor shareholders and rights of investors. The most significant growth during the period was observed in the following:

   – Transparency of government policy (from 124th to 68th place);
   – Effectiveness of work companies' boards of directors (from 123rd to 64th position).

2. Infrastructure. An increase in the country's ranking is observed in the quality of transport, electric, and phone infrastructures). Regarding the intermediate indicators, almost all of them, as in the previous case, have a positive effect: the quality of general infrastructure, quality of roads, railways, and port

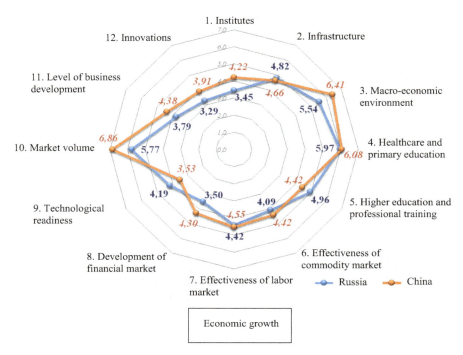

Fig. 5.1 Index of the global competitiveness of the World Economic Forum and its main components for Russia and China. *Note*: compiled by the authors on the basis of the sources (http://www.weforum.org)

infrastructure, improvement in provision of electricity and phone connections for the population. It should be noted that in 2013–2014 the largest positive results—according to the WEF specialists—were achieved in the quality of air transport infrastructure (moving from 104th to 79th position). Negative dynamics were observed for "fixed phone connection": from fifth position in 2012, Russia moved to 20th in 2014.

3. Healthcare and primary education. Over the year 2014, Russia went from 91st to 83rd position in health levels, and from 70th to 48th position in the quality of primary education.
4. Higher education and professional training. Over 2012–2014, there was growth in all intermediate indicators: provision of education and its quality, as well as training in the workplace. However, it is necessary to note the fact that the group that was viewed is problematic in some respects: there are indicators where the growth is insignificant (for the quality of its education system, Russia went up from 86th to 84th position, for the level of personnel preparation it stayed at 89th position), and there are indicators with negative growth (reduction in provision of higher education moved from 12th to 19th position; the quality of education for precise disciplines and sciences moved from 52nd to 59th). Besides, the

experts also acknowledged the fact that Russian education is worse than Chinese (in terms of quality of education system, mathematical and natural science education, management schools). Russia is also behind China in such indicators as workplace training and technological adaptation.
5. Effectiveness of commodity market. The WEF specialists noted that in competition and quality of demand terms Russia showed good growth in 2012–2014. Development of competition is related to intensification of competition in the internal market (from 124th position in 2012, Russia went to 74th in 2014), effectiveness of anti-monopoly policy (124th to 102nd), operative organization (start) of business (104th to 75th), reduction of the load of customs procedures (137th to 95th), and orientation at the client (134th to 83rd).
6. Effectiveness of labour market. Increase of the ranking is observed for labour market flexibility and effectiveness of the use of talents achieved by means of: organization of cooperation in labour relations "employer–employee" (growth for the last two years—from 125th position to 89th), flexibility in determining wages (69th to 28th), and the ratio "payment–efficiency" of labour (65th to 24th). In the indicator "ratio of women/men in labour force", there is a loss of competitiveness (38th to 41st).
7. Development of financial market. Of the two indicators of the state of the Russian financial market, the most positive is its effectiveness (68th position), as opposed to reliability and trust (125th position), though both indicators show a certain growth. Among the eight viewed intermediate indicators, seven show growth: availability and access to financial services, financing through local stock market, simple access to credit, availability of venture capital, sustainability of banks, and regulation of stock markets. Over 2012–2014, reduction in the ranking took place only for the "index of legal right" indicator (from 113th position to 118th).
8. Innovations and level of complication of factors. An increase in the country's ranking was observed in the level of development of business and for innovations. In particular, the quantity of domestic suppliers (though Russia's position is not as positive as China's) improved (from 121st position in 2012 to 91st in 2014); the quality of local suppliers (122nd to 88th); the nature of competitive advantage (125th to 75th), which indicates an increase in the level of complication of manufactured and exported products through the growth in uniqueness of products and processes; the chain of added value (129th to 96th), indicating an increase in the level of domestic companies' involvements in the process of production, sales, and distribution goods); domestic companies' control over international distribution (119th to 73rd); difficulty of production process (113th to 92nd); level of marketing development (109th to 64th); level of readiness for delegation of authorities (117th to 81st).
9. Positive dynamics are shown by a range of indicators that characterize the quality of innovational environment. In particular, over the period that was analysed, Russia increased the quality of its research and development (R&D) establishments (70th to 56th); expenses of domestic companies for R&D (79th to 62nd); significance of state purchases of leading technological products (124th

to 81st); cooperation of universities and business in the sphere of R&D (85th to 67th); the number of scientists and engineers in the country (90th to 70th); the number of patents registered (44th to 41st).

Despite the obvious development of the Russian economy and increase in the level of its national competitiveness, the WEF distinguishes a range of obvious problems.

Firstly, when studying the establishment of an innovative economy in Russia, it is impossible to omit the fact that the quality of innovative potential is decreasing: in 2012–2014, the country's ranking went down from 56th to 66th.

Secondly, there is a rather weak macro-economic environment. In fact, Russia lost ground in all intermediate indicators in 2012–2014: in particular, in the balance of the state budget (20th to 39th), in the volume of gross national savings (28th to 41st), in rates of inflation—change in the index of consumer prices (91st to 115th in 2014).

Thirdly, there is a problem with Russia's level of technological readiness. Although there is progress only with one of the two indicators included in this evaluation—technological adaptation—there is also progress at the micro-level, achieved by growth in the level of acquisition of technologies, growth in direct foreign investments, and transition of technologies. As to the second indicator—use of information and communication technologies—a reduction in competitiveness was observed in 2012–2014 (35th position to 47th). According to the specialists, the main reason for this consists of the quality and quantity of international Internet traffic calculated per capita and per number of subscribers to flexible broadband communication.

We consider that, taking all these points into account, there is a possibility that Russia could compete with such countries as Finland and Sweden which also have a large amount of natural resources. It should be noted that in 2014 Russia exceeded the countries of the BRICS (Brazil, Russia, India, China, and South Africa) as to the level of competitiveness (only being behind China) (Table 5.1). This could mean that macro-economic reforms performed in the country positively influence the Russian economy.

As for the level of competitiveness of China, and the country's advantages and disadvantages, it is necessary to note the following.

Firstly, according to the specialists' estimates, China is a more competitive country than Russia. As of year-end 2014, China was ranked 29th in the ranking of the Index of Global Competitiveness, while Russia was ranked only 53rd. Accordingly, most indicators show that modern China outperforms Russia.

In particular, the following aspects of "main components" are evaluated better in China than in Russia): level of development of institutes (both state and private); state of the macro-economic environment (excluding the balance of state budget and volume of state debt), and the level of development of the systems of healthcare and primary education.

In sub-index B, which explains the level of effectiveness of the functioning of the national economy, China's positions for the following indicators are better:

5.1 Main Directions of the Modernization of the Russian Economy in View of the...

Table 5.1 Index of global competitiveness produced by the World Economic Forum

Economy	Index of global competitiveness						
	2002–2003	2010–2011	2011–2012	2012–2013	2013–2014		2014–2015	
	Rank	Rank	Rank	Rank	Rank	Score	Rank	Score
Switzerland	7	1	1	1	1	5.67	1	5.70
Singapore	6	3	2	2	2	5.61	2	5.65
USA	2	4	5	7	5	5.48	3	5.54
Finland	1	7	4	3	3	5.54	4	5.50
Germany	13	5	6	6	4	5.51	5	5.49
Japan	11	6	9	10	9	5.40	6	5.47
Hong Kong	24	11	11	9	7	5.47	7	5.46
Netherlands	12	8	7	5	8	5.42	8	5.45
Great Britain	15	12	10	8	10	5.37	9	5.41
Sweden	3	2	3	4	6	5.48	10	5.41
China	44	27	26	29	29	4.84	28	4.89
South Africa	42	54	50	52	53	4.37	56	4.35
Brazil	54	58	53	48	56	4.33	57	4.34
India	56	51	56	59	60	4.28	71	4.21
Russia	70	63	66	67	64	4.25	53	4.37

Note: compiled by the authors on the basis of the sources (http://www.weforum.org)

organization of work of commodity market, labour market (regarding the skill of talent use), development of financial markets, and the volumes of internal and external markets.

In turn, in part of sub-index C, which is responsible for the level of development of innovations and the complication of factors that occur in the countries, China's positions for all indicators are higher than Russia's. Thus, it is necessary to note the following aspects of China's economy, and changes between 2012 and 2014:

- Progress in competitive advantage (56th position to 45th), which (as in Russia's case) shows the increase in the level of complication of manufactured and exported products by means of the growing uniqueness of the products and processes used;
- Complication of the added value chain (49th to 37th). This growth shows an increase in the level of involvement of domestic companies in the process of manufacture, sales, and distribution of products;
- Increase in the level of control of domestic companies over international distribution (41st to 31st);
- Growth in the quality of research institutes (44th to 39th);
- Growing revenues of domestic companies for the conduct of R&D (23rd to 22nd);
- Strengthening of cooperation of universities and business in the sphere of R&D (35th to 32nd);
- Increase in significance of state purchases of leading technological products for the country's economy (16th to 10th);
- Growth in the number of patents registered in the country (38th to 34th).

Summing up the data, the following conclusions may be reached.

Firstly, Russia, as a country that lags behind China in most aspects of national competitiveness, should—together with "independent work on mistakes" (modernization of its economy)—try to involve in the realization of its own interests China's competitive advantages. In other words, while perfecting its strategy of foreign economic relations, Russia should not abandon China's better and reliable commodity market, its labour market, or its financial market, as these Chinese internal markets are larger than the Russian ones. Most importantly, Russia should actively use the innovative potential of China to organize joint business and follow commodity flows.

Secondly, Russia should pay attention to where it still exceeds China on competitiveness and try to use this information when making decisions about the direction of Russian–Chinese cooperation. The areas noted include higher level of technological preparedness, level of development of higher education (in part the coverage of the country's population), and quality of electricity and phone infrastructure.

In other words, Russia should avoid international competition in the wide areas of sectorial development which are difficult for its economy. It is necessary to determine horizons for further development by using the gigantic possibilities of peaceful foreign economic interaction with leading innovation complexes (in the

5.1 Main Directions of the Modernization of the Russian Economy in View of the...

context of our work, China's innovation complex) for the purpose of modernizing the country's economy by means of mutually profitable initiatives and its technical re-equipment (Jahfer and Inoue 2014).

An understandable question might arise. Why, viewing the topic of activation of foreign trade relations between Russia and China, are you deviating from the sphere of foreign economic cooperation towards internal economic development of the state?" In our opinion, the answer is obvious. The internal economic component is a driving force for the country's development as a whole, and for its trade component in particular. Before offering something in the global market and occupying that niche through the processes of international division of labour, it should be produced (alone or in cooperation). In the case of modern Russia, cooperation is a way out of a dead-end situation, where it turns into a raw materials periphery or half-periphery for the world's developed countries. Cooperation with China is a real chance of not only increasing the ranking of national competitiveness but keeping the country in modern geo-political and geo-economic environments, and as one of the most significant global powers.

Our approach to correcting the structure of Russia's foreign trade includes determining the factors which are the basis of structural changes for Russia's foreign trade, setting the goals and key tasks, methods, means, and variants of changes, and all these, as well as its potential results, are given in Fig. 5.2.

Let us emphasize that in speaking of the possibility of expanding cooperation between Russia and China we do not view the Russian extractive sphere of the economy as continuing to specialize in the export of raw materials and products with a low level of processing; this would simply involve spending the country's national wealth (which is exhaustible) in the global market, without any improvement or growth in internal potential. Besides, the necessity for the country to leave pure raw materials export specialization was emphasized again by the global situation, related to the reduction in oil prices in 2014.

The topic of the discussion is the process by which the processing sector of Russia's economy is modernized through innovation. The problem is that the state of those products manufactured in Russia (and supplied for export, including into China) with a higher level of processing (as compared to raw materials) could be characterized as unfavourable. In other words, improving the existing commodity structure of exports by increasing the level of processing and increasing the quality of exported products is a primary task, which should be promoted to the rank of state programme.

It should be noted that this is already being done in Russia and China; a rich normative and legal base for the establishment and development of an innovative economy is already being created.

Investment projects and the participation of foreign investors in such projects in Russia are regulated by a series of federal laws: No. 160-FZ dated 9 July 1999 "On foreign investment in the Russian Federation" (determining the main guarantees of rights of foreign investors), No. 225-FZ dated 30 December 1995 "On agreements for products division" (regulating activities in the sphere of prospecting and extraction of mineral deposits in Russia according to the terms of agreements on

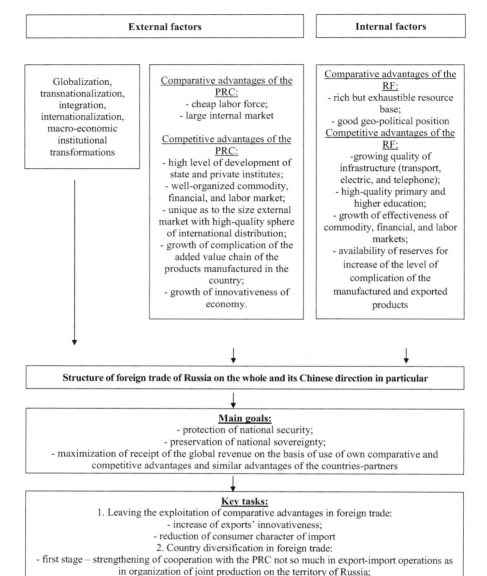

Fig. 5.2 Directions of correction of Russia's foreign trade. *Note*: offered by the authors

5.1 Main Directions of the Modernization of the Russian Economy in View of the... 85

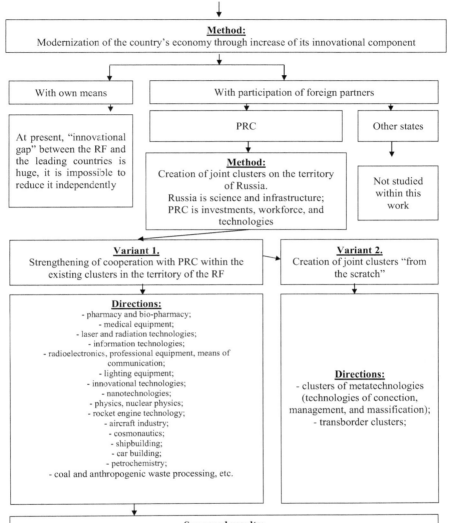

Fig. 5.2 (continued)

product processing), No. 39-FZ dated 25 February 1999 "On investment activities in the Russian Federation, conducted in the form of capital investments", No. 173-FZ dated 10 December 2003 "On currency regulation and currency control", No. 115-FZ dated 21 July 2005 "On concessional contracts", No. 116 dated 22 July 2005 "On special economic areas in the Russian Federation", No. 57-FZ dated 29 April 2008 "On the order of conduct of foreign investments into economic societies with a strategic role for protection of the country and security of the state" (regulating activities in strategic spheres). Also relevant are the Agreement on the issues of free (special) economic areas on customs territory of the Customs Union and custom procedure of free custom zone dated 18 June 2016, and Civil and Tax Codes.

Based on the accumulated global experience of establishing innovative economies, the most widespread tool is clusters. These allow the creation of national innovative fields that are adequate for the needs of modern global markets.

The cluster policy in Russia is conducted according to the "Concept of long-term socio-economic development of the Russian Federation until 2020" and the "Strategy of innovational development of the Russian Federation until 2020", which suggest the creation of territorial and reproduction clusters through the use of competitive potential, and the development of innovative high-tech products aimed at increasing the level of processing of natural resources, an increase in the localization of assembly production, import substitution, and an increase in competitiveness for the Russian economy.

To this end, state programmes were developed: "Development of industry and increase of its competitiveness", "Development of aviation industry", "Space activities of Russia", "Development of pharmaceutical and medical industry", "Development of shipbuilding", "Development of electronic and radio electronic industry", and "Development of agriculture and regulation of the markets of agricultural products, raw materials, and food". These should be correlated to the programmes of development in territorial innovation clusters.

Moreover, according to Russian laws,[3] the following measures of state support for the development of innovational territorial clusters are supposed:

- Providing subsidized budgets for the realization of measures envisaged by the programmes of development in territorial innovation clusters;

---

[3]Federal Law dated 24July 2007 No. 209-FZ "On development of small and medium entrepreneurship in the Russian Federation", Decree of the Government of the Russian Federation dated 6 March 2013 No. 188 "On establishment of the Rules of distribution and provision of subsidies from the federal budget to the budgets of the subjects of the Russian Federation for realization of measures envisaged by the programmes of development of pilot innovational territorial clusters", and the Order of the Ministry of Economic Development of Russia dated 25 March No. 167 "On establishment of terms of competitive selection of the subjects of the Russian Federation which budgets receive subsidies from the federal budget for state support of small and medium entrepreneurship, including farm enterprises, and requirements to organizations which create the infrastructure of support for subjects of small and medium entrepreneurship".

- Supporting measures related to territorial innovation clusters within federal targeted programmes and state programmes;
- Attracting state-instituted development towards the realization of programmes of development for territorial innovation clusters;
- Attracting companies in which the state participates, to help them realize programmes of innovative development in territorial innovation clusters;
- Applying territorial innovation clusters using part of the tax that was envisaged for Skolkovo. The innovational center "Skolkovo" (Moscow) is a modern scientific and technological complex for development and commercialization of new technologies.

According to the Federal Law dated 6 October 1999 No. 184-FZ "On general principles of organization of legal (representative) and executive bodies of state power of the subjects of the Russian Federation", the development of territorial innovation clusters includes:

- Organizing and conducting regional scientific, technical, and innovative programmes and projects, including by Russian scientific organizations;
- Solving the issues of organization and conduct of regional and intermunicipal programmes and projects as they affect the development of small and medium entrepreneurial businesses;
- Organizing and conducting intermunicipal investment projects and investment projects aimed at developing the social and engineering infrastructure of municipal entities.

According to the "Strategy of innovational development of the Russian Federation until 2020", the bodies of state power and local government shall support the development of territorial innovation clusters in the following ways:

- Support for the institutional development of clusters (creation of an organization for the development of territorial innovation clusters, strategic planning for the development of clusters, effective cooperation between cluster members);
- Development of mechanisms of support for projects that are aimed at increasing the competitiveness of enterprises and support for the effectiveness of their interactions (stimulating innovations and developing mechanisms through which technologies are commercialized, increasing the quality of management in cluster enterprises, and increasing the competitiveness of products, supporting the marketing of products, and attracting direct investment);
- Provision of favourable conditions for the development of clusters (reduction in administrative barriers, provision of tax subsidies, investments into innovational infrastructure, development of professional education, and cooperation between education and production).

This process is already active in Russia. According to the Order of the Prime-Minister of the Russian Federation dated 28 August 2012 No. DM-P8-5060, a list of 25 territorial innovational clusters has been established (Table 5.2).

Table 5.2 List of innovation clusters in Russia

Federal district	Territorial location	Specialization of cluster
Siberian	Altai Krai	Pharmacy and biotechnologies
	Kemerovo Oblast	Processing of coal and anthropogenic waste
	Krasnoyarsk Krai	Innovational technologies (Zheleznogorsk)
	Novosibirsk Oblast	Information technologies, pharmacy, biotechnologies
	Tomsk Oblast	Information technologies, pharmacy, and medical equipment
Northwestern	St Petersburg	Information technologies, radio electronics, professional equipment, communication means and telecommunications
	St Petersburg	Medical and pharmaceutical industries, radiation technologies
	Arkhangelsk Oblast	Shipbuilding
Central	Moscow Oblast	New materials, laser and radiation technologies (Troitsk)
	Moscow	Machine building, microelectronics, and nanotechnologies
	Kaluga Oblast	Pharmacy, biotechnologies, and biomedicine
	Moscow Oblast	Biotechnologies
	Moscow Oblast	Cluster "Phys-tech XXI" (Dolgoprudniy, Khimki)
	Moscow Oblast	Nuclear physics and nanotechnologies (Dubna)
Volga	Nizhny Novgorod Oblast	Car building and petrochemistry
	Nizhny Novgorod Oblast	Professional equipment, micro-electronics, nanotechnologies, and new materials
	Perm Krai	Rocket engine building
	Republic of Bashkortostan	Petrochemistry
	Republic of Mordovia	Energy effective sources of light, lighting equipment, and intellectual systems of lighting management
	Republic of Tatarstan	Petrochemistry, oil refining, and car industry
	Samara Oblast	Rocket and space production and aircraft industry
	Ulyanovsk Oblast	Aircraft industry
	Ulyanovsk Oblast	Nuclear technologies (Dimitrovgrad)
Ural	Sverdlovsk Oblast	Titanium cluster
Far Eastern	Khabarovsk Krai	Aircraft industry and shipbuilding

Note: compiled by the authors on the basis of the sources (http://gtmarket.ru/ratings/global-innovation-index/info)

Despite the fact that direct participants in these structural entities are only currently Russian economic agents, the work of a range of clusters supposes active cooperation with such countries as India, China, and Israel. In particular, Chinese enterprises are Russia's active partners in the chemical and pharmaceutical industry, the car industry, metallurgy, nuclear energy, and forestry. In addition, products from these clusters are aimed not only at the internal market but also at China and countries in Southeast Asia.

Based on the modern tendencies in the development of the global economy, a growing share of cooperative operations in the international division of labour, and the strengthening of the role of foreign investments in the development of national economies, we think that Russia should let China enter its existing clusters and also help to create new clusters on the basis of parity: Russia would provide science and infrastructure, and China would provide investments, workforce, and technologies (based on the competitive advantages that have been determined).

This conclusion is based on a range of factors.

Firstly, by cooperating with China, Russia will gain experience of work in this sector of development of the national economy. The Chinese have already taken that path—and have done so rather successfully. They required 15 years to create competitive clusters from scratch. The spheres in which they operated were not selected randomly but on the basis of existing growth areas: the textile industry, sports products, clothing, toys, crockery, for example. Based on this, it would be wise to attract the Chinese to create joint clusters for areas that are interesting for China, where Russia still has a competitive advantage, such as machine building, shipbuilding, communications, tourism, education, healthcare, and agribusiness.[4] Joint clustering of these spheres is supported by the fact that the products are able to access global markets.

Secondly, creation of clusters in these spheres will allow them to increase their importance in Russia. In the development of international business, we are losing out not only to the developed countries, but to the BRICS countries (Brazil, Russia, India, China, and South Africa) as well. The specialization of successful Russian transnational corporations (TNCs) is strictly limited to such sectors as energy, metallurgy, and telecommunications. However, despite the significance of the companies that work in those spheres in terms of the Russian economy, even they lag behind their main rivals with regard to many indicators that determine their place and role in the global market (capitalization, sales volume, profit, and effectiveness). Thus, for example, one of Russia's largest oil extracting companies Lukoil OJSC is 5.5 times behind such oil corporations as Exxon Mobil Corporation

---

[4]According to the World Economic Forum and Harvard University experts' estimates, modern Russia has very strong international positions in fuel and energy sector and iron industry; strong positions—in nonferrous metallurgy, petrochemistry, timber and military industries; medium positions—in chemistry, car building and shipbuilding, general machine building, and professional equipment; weak positions—in civil aircraft industry, electronics, and textile industry (Jahfer and Inoue 2014).

(USA) with regard to sales volumes, 2.5 times behind Petrobras (Brazil), and 1.6 times behind PetroChina and Sinopec China Petroleum (Jahfer and Inoue 2014).

As to effectiveness (according to estimates), Russian corporations are behind the Americans and Europeans (by 3 times) and certain Chinese corporations (by 1.6 times). As for domestic enterprises which function in other spheres of the Russian economy, despite obvious comparative advantages they cannot compete in global markets in terms of price or quality. For example, in machine building, Russia is behind the global leaders by two technological generations, each of which is 10–15 years long.

As the strategic directions of cooperation between the two countries are developed, it is necessary to determine, apart from the subjects mentioned above, the joint work that will take place within new clusters regarding the creation of meta-technologies. Currently, the Russian and Chinese sides are both interested in generating modern technologies of communication and technologies of management and massification, possession of which excludes any competition.[5]

It is possible that newly created clusters will have a transborder character; in other words, they will be located in two places simultaneously but united by a common economic existence.

Thirdly, by cooperating with China, Russia will receive access to higher level technologies, modern tools of management, and existing infrastructure.

Fourthly, it will be possible to progress from the consumer character of Russian imports. Instead of importing equipment that is necessary to improve competitiveness, we import finished essential goods, such as clothing and footwear. It should be emphasized that cooperation with the Chinese will mean that the clusters will be able to produce necessary technological equipment, or that their direct supply from China will be possible through joint enterprises.

Fifthly, we can reduce the existing gap between Russia and leading countries as regards the level of innovative capability of the state and its subjects. There is a huge difference between the level of development of science and education in Russia and the innovative capability of its subjects: it is possible to possess a unique system of education and a scientific base and at the same time to have no innovative potential (as in Russia's case) and, on the contrary, to be able to create new technologies but not be a leader in education or scientific research (as in China's case). Besides, it is necessary to take into account the fact that Russia is gradually losing its position (as compared with China) in the scientific sphere.

In particular, comparing the level of educational development, Russia is obviously ahead of China: it is the largest intellectual treasury of the world and holds a higher position in the average level of education (Tables 5.3 and 5.4).

---

[5]Currently, seven developed countries possess 46 out of 50 meta-technologies which ensure competitive production, while the rest of the world possesses only three or four of them. The USA has 20–22 meta-technologies (Germany 8–10, Japan 7, England and France 3–5, Sweden, Norway, Italy, and Switzerland 1–2 each) (Jahfer and Inoue 2014).

5.1 Main Directions of the Modernization of the Russian Economy in View of the... 91

Table 5.3 Ranking of Russia and China on the index of education, 1980–2013

Country	1980	1990	2000	2005	2010	2013
Russia	0.576	0.660	0.723	0.764	0.780	0.780
China	0.358	0.406	0.478	0.531	0.599	0.610

Note: compiled by the authors on the basis of the sources (Human Development Report 2014)

Table 5.4 Value of criteria for the evaluation of the level of education in Russia and China (HDI calculation methodology) in 2014

Indicator	Russia	China
Gross coefficient of education coverage: pre-school education (% of pre-school age children)	90.0	62.0
Gross coefficient of education coverage: primary education (% of primary schoolers)	99.0	128.0
Gross coefficient of education coverage: secondary education (% of children of secondary schoolers)	85.0	87.0
Gross coefficient of education coverage: higher education (% of population of tertiary school age)	75.0	24.0
Without primary education (% of the contingent of primary school)	3.85	No data
Population covered at least by secondary education (%, age 25+)	90.9	65.3
Level of literacy of adult population (%, age 15+)	99.7	95.1
Average number of years of study at school	11.73	7.54
Expected number of years of study at school	14.0	12.9
Student–teacher ratio	18	17
Expenses for education (% of GDP)	4.0	No data

Note: compiled by the authors on the basis of the sources (http://www.opec.org)

However, as with scientific research, the numbers show that modern Russia spends less on science than China—both in relative and absolute terms (Table 5.5).

As to the level of R&D activity, determined by the National Scientific Fund of the USA as the total number of R&D articles published in the peer-reviewed scientific journals that are indexed in the Science Citation Index (SCI) and Social Sciences Citation Index (SSCI), Russia is also far behind China (Table 5.6).[6]

The situation is even worse in the sphere of innovation: modern China is ranked 29th and Russia only 49th on the index of innovations (Table 5.7). This indicator is a weighted average sum of evaluations of the following indicators:

- Existing resources and conditions for conduct of innovations (institutes, human capital, infrastructure, development of internal market and business);
- Achieved practical results of innovations (development of technologies and economy of knowledge, results of creative activities).

---

[6]Analysis of scientific and research publications covers the following spheres: earth sciences, astronomy and space, mathematics, physics, chemistry, medicine, psychology, sociology, technology, machine building, and agricultural sciences (http://www.weforum.org).

Table 5.5 Ranking of countries for the level of expenses for R&D in 2012

R&D in relative terms			Absolute expenses for R&D	
Position	Country	Expenses, % of GDP	Country	Expenses, $ million
1	Israel	4.4	USA	454,859.2
2	Finland	3.88	Japan	200,246.5
3	South Korea	3.74	China	139,860.8
4	Sweden	3.40	Germany	95,868.4
5	Japan	3.36	France	58,789.8
6	Denmark	3.06	Great Britain	42,859.1
7	Switzerland	2.99	South Korea	42,247.0
8	USA	2.90	Brazil	26,130.9
9	Germany	2.82	Italy	25,367.1
10	Austria	2.75	Russia	23,371.4
21	China	1.70	Austria	10,990.3
32	Russia	1.16	Denmark	9615.8

Note: compiled by the authors on the basis of the sources (http://gtmarket.ru/ratings/research-and-development-expenditure/info)

Table 5.6 Ranking of countries for the level of R&D activities, 2012–2014

		Number of articles	
Position (2012/2014)	Country	2012	2014
1/1	USA	208,601	212,394.2
2/2	China	74,019	89,894.4
3/3	Japan	49,627	47,105.7
4/5	Great Britain	45,649	46,035.4
5/4	Germany	45,003	46,258.8
6/6	France	31,748	31,685.5
7/7	Canada	29,017	29,113.7
8/8	Italy	26,755	26,503.4
9/9	South Korea	22,271	25,592.7
10/10	Spain	21,543	22,910.3
14/15	Russia	14,016	14,150.9

Note: compiled by the authors on the basis of the sources (http://gtmarket.ru/ratings/scientific-and-technical-activity/info)

Based on the above, we consider that by expanding Russian–Chinese cooperation in the creation and perfection of Russian clusters, Russia can neutralize its weak spots, raise the level of national and commodity competitiveness, and change the commodity structure of foreign trade operations, including with China.

In its turn, China will receive access to the Russian market for services through the fulfilment of joint infrastructural projects (in the transport sphere, and in the extraction and processing of natural resources), and the execution of service contracts and contracted works with the attraction of Chinese capital and workforce. It will also profit from the completion of joint investment projects in Russia; the import of products manufactured by joint investment projects; access to Russian

Table 5.7 Ranking of countries in the index of innovations, 2012–2014

Country	2012 Position	Ranking	2013 Position	Ranking	2014 Position	Ranking
Switzerland	1	68.2	1	66.6	1	64.8
Sweden	2	64.8	2	6.4	3	62.3
Singapore	3	63.5	8	59.4	7	59.2
Finland	4	61.8	6	59.5	4	60.7
Great Britain	5	61.2	3	61.2	2	62.4
Netherlands	6	60.5	4	61.1	5	60.6
USA	10	57.7	5	60.3	6	60.1
China	34	45.4	35	44.7	29	46.6
Russia	51	37.9	62	37.2	49	39.1

Note: compiled by the authors on the basis of the sources (http://gtmarket.ru/news/2014/07/18/6841)

scientific developments and technologies; and from the possibility of joint scientific and technical research, and the industrial implementation of the results.

5.2 Measures of State Regulation and Cooperation for the Realization of Russia's Economic Interests in Foreign Trade Cooperation with China

To determine and develop measures for state regulation and support the realization of Russia's economic interests in foreign trade cooperation with China, it is necessary to study the experience of China, which has achieved huge success in the development of its national economy and foreign trade.

Today, foreign trade plays a large role in the development of China's economy. Among the advantages taken from the active development of relevant activities, China has eventually created the necessary conditions for further national economic growth: it has expanded the sales market of domestic products (and those manufactured within TNCs); attracted and used in the country the export revenue raised; expanded the range of products offered in the internal market; received access to resources, global scientific achievements, and technologies which are hard to find internally; and has created new jobs in export-oriented spheres of the national economy.

In the late 1990s, the foreign trade turnover of China constituted $500 billion annually. With a current turnover of $4.1 trillion, China has changed from a country that imported capital and technologies from abroad into one of the leaders of the global economy, which exports capital and final products, including high-tech.

Constant growth in the volume of imports (after China entered the World Trade Organization (WTO) in 2001, its annual growth has exceeded $100 billion) provides the Chinese economy with necessary raw materials and is an important means for borrowing leading foreign technologies.

Table 5.8 Dynamics of China's foreign exchange reserves in 2005–2015

Year	2005	2006	2007	2008	2009	2010	2011	2012	2013	2014	2015
$ billion	818	1066	1528	1946	2399	2847	3253	3379	3880	3843	3406

Note: compiled by the authors on the basis of the sources (http://www.mof.gov.cn)

Owing to growing trade profits (over 1990–2013, the export surplus of China grew from $10.7 billion to $259.0 billion) and inflow of foreign investments, the country has increased its foreign-exchange reserves. As of December 2015, these reached $3406 billion (Table 5.8). As a comparison, it may be noted that Russia's foreign-exchange reserves constituted $377.8 billion at that time.

At the time of writing, China is ranked first in the world as regards the volume of foreign-exchange reserves, which allows it (with annual imports worth $1.9 trillion) to support imports for two years, which is significantly higher than the level recommended by the IMF (International Monetary Fund).[7] Such a high level of foreign-exchange reserves allowed China to overcome the global financial crisis with minimal losses. Besides, according to Antoine and Guischar, a large volume of foreign trade profit of China and its foreign-exchange reserves guarantee the country free access to global natural resources. Contracts for long-term supplies in China for direct control over raw materials deposits have been concluded all over the world. "This includes Russia, Central Asia, Iran, and other countries of Middle-East, Africa, of which one may say 'China purchases Africa', and Latin America—especially Venezuela, Chile, and Brazil which is in the process of negotiations regarding the contract for development of a rich deposit on the shelf not far from Rio-de-Janeiro. This strategy is rather successful: not only China comes into possession of natural deposits of the countries which were previously in the orbit of the Western countries but also risks the intrusion into certain spheres of the Western countries or in the direct proximity. Ten years ago, China's extracting oil on the shelf of the Gulf of Mexico was unthinkable!" (Galbraith 2015, p. 161).

Based on the current situation, we can consider the key factors that have played an important role in the process of development of China's foreign trade activities.

Firstly, there is the wise choice of foreign trade policy, preparing its strategic and normative and legal basis, and creating the conditions necessary for transformation of foreign economic activities.

We consider that a strategically important step for the development of China's economy was refusing protectionism in foreign trade, and Deng Xiaoping's government's selection of an export-oriented model for the country's development in 1979.

China, in order to regulate the volume and quality of foreign trade operations, began to use quotas and direct subsidies for specific spheres of industry (production of clothing, computer equipment, electrical equipment and spare parts, production

---

[7]The IMF's recommendations determine the minimum level of foreign-exchange reserves, which allow the provision of the import of goods and services for three months (http://www.imf.org).

5.2 Measures of State Regulation and Cooperation for the Realization of... 95

of telecommunication technology goods) by provision of subsidies and tax subsidies. When China entered the WTO in 2001, custom charges were significantly reduced. In April 1996, import taxes were reduced from 35 % to 23 % for 5000 items, in October 1997 from 23 % to 17 % for 4900 items, and in January 2001 from 17.0 % to 15.3 % for 3500 items; this was the main basis for all taxes and fees. Thus, the level of import taxes for industrial products constitutes up to 10 %.

Within the export-oriented model, the strategy of developing foreign trade activities was passed in the late 1990s at state level. Because the rate of economic growth exceeded internal consumption and led to deflation, the government made a decision for the more active orientation of Chinese manufacturers towards the export of products and capital. Thus, beginning in 1997, China has stuck to the strategy called "Going beyond", which is aimed at the active movement of national manufacturers to external markets. The purpose of this strategy was the quadrupling of China's GDP by 2020, and by 2020–2030 the establishment of China as the world's largest economy.

This strategy is based on using the advantages of two markets and two raw materials resources (internal and external), by means of which China received substantial possibilities for economic development and optimization of its expenses (Столярова 2009) (Fig. 5.3).

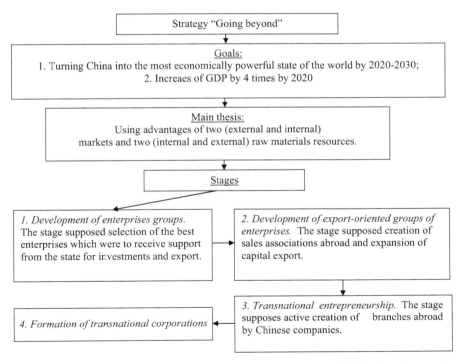

Fig. 5.3 Realization of the PRC's strategy "Going beyond". *Note*: compiled by the authors on the basis of the sources (Ma and Ma 2000)

Eventually, the government counted on the stimulation of domestic enterprises through the export of final products, the expansion of manufactured products, entering new foreign markets, attracting innovational technologies into the Chinese economy, starting to acquire natural resources in foreign states, and the creation of TNCs, which manufactured products that were able to compete in the global market. For this, the strategy envisaged an expansion in the volume of investments abroad.

The main driving force during realization of this strategy was private enterprises, which were encouraged to create joint enterprises with foreign companies related to innovational developments and new technologies, to participate in the transfer of technologies, and to attract Chinese citizens to help complete various construction projects in other countries.

Four stages were distinguished within the strategy—as is illustrated in Fig. 3.1. Between 2000 and 2010, the first two stages were realized. Beginning in 2005, the Ministry of Commerce and the Ministry of Finance provided state support for particular foreign economic sectors (agriculture, forestry, fishing industry, and innovative technologies).

Special attention was also given to the creation of branches and subsidiaries of Chinese companies abroad, as well as joint enterprises, in order to increase the export of Chinese products and to bring to fruition various foreign investment projects in the spheres of infrastructure, extraction, natural resources, and so on. Chinese investments were mainly directed towards the countries of Asia, Africa, and Western Europe (Ma Weigang 2000).

It should be noted that creating foreign offices for branches of Chinese companies was accompanied by the movement of entrepreneurs and workers from China into other countries. With the expansion of Chinese communities abroad, in 2000 the work of the Department for Overseas Chinese of the State Council of China was activated; this was conducted within the "labour directions" section of the "Going beyond" strategy, as communities have to stimulate creation of favourable conditions in the countries of residence for Chinese enterprises that are entering foreign markets and support the realization of China's foreign economic strategy abroad (Isabel 2015).

A second, no less important, factor which determines scale and specifics of foreign trade activities in China is the use—as the basis for building foreign economic activities—not of hypothetical competitive advantages that conform to the key tendencies of the development global economy, which are created by the state, but comparative advantages which are "given by nature".

Here we speak of a cheap workforce, of which China has plenty.

As part of the reforms conducted in the 1980s–1990s, it was decided that labour resources of the country should be used not only in domestic enterprises; but because of their relatively low cost, they could perform key roles in the process of transnationalization in leading countries. China uses the policy of active

Table 5.9 Dynamics of direct foreign investments into China's economy

Year	1990	1995	2000	2005	2010	2014
$ billion	3.5	35.8	38.4	104.1	243.7	289.1

Note: compiled by the authors on the basis of the sources (http://www.crc.mofcom.gov.cn/crweb/rcc/info/Article.jsp?col_no=107&a_no=237022)

attraction of foreign capital—mainly in the form of direct investments. A corresponding reform of the legal system is under way.[8]

The exposure of China's economy to the global market started from the moment when attractive conditions were created for the inflow of foreign capital. As a result, the country became one of the global leaders in terms of the rates and volumes of foreign capital's involvement in the national economy; the share of high-tech products in exports was quickly increased by means of foreign investments.

The high effectiveness of the reforms that were conducted in the sphere of laws aimed at attracting foreign investments is proved by the growth in volume of foreign investments in China's economy. In 1990–2013, the volume of direct foreign investments into China grew from $3.5 billion to $289.1 billion (Table 5.9). As to the volume of attracted foreign investments, China is ranked second in the world.

A third factor that positively influenced the development of foreign trade activities in China is the country's policy to create free economic areas (FEAs). For the purpose of stimulating the development of export-oriented areas in China in the 1980s, free trade areas were created in Guangzhou, Dalian, Ningbo, Xiamen, Tianjin, Fuzhou, Haikou, Qingdao, Zhangjiagang, Zhuhai, Shanghai, Shantou, and Shenzhen. Today, in addition to FEAs, there is a range of administrative entities in China, the residents of which are excused from export and import custom taxes and are able to perform payments either in yuans or in foreign currency.[9]

Apart from free trade areas, high-technology areas with developed infrastructure and modern equipment were created. The Chinese government views science and technology as a key factor in the economic development of the country, and the creation of high-tech areas, which provided support for venture entrepreneurs in the form of tax subsidies and subsidies for the rental of premises, allowed progress in this direction [Ли Хуа Китайская открытая стратегия экономического развития 2001, pp. 35–37].

---

[8]Three new laws were passed: the law on enterprises with a share of foreign capital; the law on joint enterprises with the participation of foreign companies; and the law on companies with 100 % foreign capital. In 1994, the law on companies was passed (http://www.mof.gov.cn).

[9]There are 32 areas of economic and technological development in Beijing, Shanghai, Guangzhou, Tianjin, Dalian, Harbin, Ürümqi, Wuhan, Chongqing, Hangzhou, Shenyang, Changchun, Yingkou, and other large cities; and 14 areas of transborder economic cooperation in Dandong, Heihe, Suifenhe (Heilongjiang province), Erenhot, Huichun (Jilin province), Yining City, Tacheng, Pingxiang, Dongxing, Ruili, and Hekou (Yunnan province) [Ли Хуа Китайская открытая стратегия экономического развития 2007, pp. 35–37].

Nowadays, China strives for access to important and key technologies, through, for example, the development of scientific and technical potential (foreign investments are attracted into high-tech spheres, subsidies for national developers and manufacturers of innovative products are provided, and highly qualified specialists from abroad are attracted.

An important fact is that the functioning of FEAs, as well as a wise regional policy, leads to a transformation of the regional structure of foreign trade activities. In particular, western and central regions started moving towards external markets more actively. Thus, the general volume of foreign trade turnover in the western and central provinces exceeded ¥240 billion, or $36.5 billion (growth of more than 40 %). There is a gradual levelling of the regional structure of export, and imbalances in the country's economy are eliminated. The traditional drivers of foreign trade of China were Shanghai and Beijing, but recently an active role in foreign trade operations has been played by five industrially developed provinces of the south and east coast. Foreign trade is also apparent in central and western provinces (the Tibet Autonomous Region became a leader in its growth rate, exceeding even the Sichuan province with regard to the absolute indicators).

Finally, another important factor that determines the significant place that is occupied by China in the sphere of foreign trade is the policy of a reduced currency rate.

Global experience shows that this policy leads to the artificial reduction of prices in the global market for goods manufactured in the country, which positively influences exports.

From the point of view of the theory of international economy, an appreciation in national currency leads to a growth in prices for export products, which leads to a reduction in competitiveness and reduction of supplies of domestic products in the global market, and therefore import growth because of the relative reduction of prices; as a result of this the country's trade balance becomes worse. The opposite tendency is observed during currency depreciation.

It is possible to note that a growth in yuan rate leads to opposite reactions to a growth in China's imports. Thus, it is possible to distinguish a range of countries (Saudi Arabia, Brazil, and India), for which the growth of import volumes in China depends on yuan appreciation and on a reduction of custom taxes in China. This allows for the supposition that products from these countries (goods from Brazil and India, oil and oil products from Saudi Arabia under the Chinese government's policy of diversification of energy supply) may receive competitive advantages in China's internal market.

In other studied countries, appreciation of the yuan means reduction of volumes of imports to China. This could be explained by the fact that products of these countries are mainly represented by components and investment goods of TNCs, goods imported according to long-term contracts, and goods provided according to one-off contracts. To the fullest extent this is apparent in the ASEAN countries (Association of Southeast Asian Nations), Hong Kong, and Taiwan, and least of all in the USA, Australia, the EU, Russia, Japan, and Republic of Korea.

State measures include stage-by-stage liberalization of the foreign economic sphere and the restructuring of the economy, attracting foreign capital, developing export-oriented national production (initially, capital- and science intensive final industrial products), diversification of sales markets, entering the WTO, creation of FEAs and areas of development of new and high technologies. All these measures have allowed China to become one of the leaders of the global economy.

Despite the fact that China's experience of developing foreign trade has a positive effect on developing Russia's foreign trade activities and the activation of Russian–Chinese foreign trade cooperation, in order to modernize the Russian economy, it is necessary to take into account possible threats that might appear if growing cooperation with China takes place. These are:

- Further preservation of the existing commodity structure of export of raw materials resources from Russia, with food products and products of mass consumption being imported from China. This makes the Russian economy dependent on the dynamics of the raw materials export sphere and demand for raw materials from China, and will simulate further outflow of highly qualified specialists from Siberia and the Far East;
- Formation of export flows of raw materials with direct connection to China, without the creation of a diversified structure of sales, which makes China a monopolistic buyer that is able to dictate terms on the basis of its interests (e.g., the tough position of China on the pricing of oil supplied through the Eastern Siberia–Pacific Ocean oil pipeline and natural gas supplied through the Power of Siberia pipeline);
- China's participation in the realization of projects in Russia that are aimed at the extraction and export of raw materials resources, without their preliminary processing or the manufacture of products with high level of value added, as well as tough exploitation of Russian agricultural land for the export of agricultural products;
- Processing products in Russia (forestry, gas and oil refining, metallurgy, etc.), and raw materials based on the resources of the Siberian and Far-Eastern regions, as well as China's opposition to certain projects that are related to the development and modernization of product refining in Russia;
- Creation of technological dependence on China during the realization of joint infrastructural projects—because sanctions are imposed on Russia, and these hinder the receipt of technologies and equipment from industrially developed countries;
- The dependence of the Russian economy on Chinese capital (e.g., because of terms of provision of credit assets in connection with the purchase of Chinese technologies, equipment, and products, as well as attraction of workforce from China), owing to sanctions regarding Russia imposed by Western countries;
- Aggravation of problems related to the increase in the number of migrants from China, owing to the demographic conditions in transborder regions of the Russian Far East and the Chinese north-eastern regions, including the growth of unemployment;

- Copying Russian technologies (military and aerospace in particular) without their licensing, including for the manufacture of export products, which leads to rivalry with Russian products in the global markets;
- Completing the Eurasian Land Bridge infrastructural project without using Russian territory might lead to reductions in traffic on the Baikal–Amur mainline, the Trans-Siberian Railway, and the Northeast Passage.

Thus, in conclusion, we consider that in view of China's experience in the development of foreign economic activities and Russia's readiness to deepen foreign trade connections with China in order to minimize possible threats and serve Russia's national economic interests in its interactions with China, there is a necessity to create a series of state regulations for foreign trade between the two countries within Russian law (Fig. 5.4):

- Creation of free trade areas and innovation clusters (with the provision of privileged regimes for foreign partners) in order to develop and modernize processing industrial enterprises in directions that will allow a multiplicative effect for Russian industry (this is primarily for metallurgy and machine building);
- Organization of effective control over the preservation of ecological norms in agriculture when agricultural land is being provided for rent (at the moment there is no such control, and provision of agricultural land for long-term rent to Chinese enterprises is not well received in Russian society);
- Expansion of interaction in joint scientific, technical, experimental, and industrial development;
- Preservation of the technological superiority of the Russian military complex, which will allow Russia to have a competitive advantage in the case of illegal copying and global marketing of Russian technologies;
- Attraction of foreign workforce only on a temporary basis, according to issued quotas (such measures were used during preparations for the APEC (Asia-Pacific Economic Cooperation) summit in Vladivostok) and organization of effective migration and transborder control;
- Expansion of mutually profitable cooperation between Russia and countries of the Asia-Pacific Region (political, economic, and technological) within international organizations (APEC, BRICS, the Shanghai Cooperation Organisation, etc.) and between two parties, in order to balance the interests of Russia, China, and other countries of the Asia-Pacific Region and to preserve Russia's independent position in the world.
- Support for Russian manufacturers—financial and non-tariff (as within the WTO, Russian cannot increase taxes). Financial support might be in the form of provision of state subsidies, tax subsidies and tax breaks, reduction of interest rates for credit, and organization of state purchases of products. Non-tariff support might be in the form of stiffening of technical standards for certain types of products (e.g., Chinese polyvinyl chloride, which is low quality but is cheaper than Russian product; the same situation occurs with Chinese cement, the use of which leads to a reduction in quality and security of constructed

5.2 Measures of State Regulation and Cooperation for the Realization of... 101

Long-term goals of socio-economic development of Russia:
– modernization of national economy and increase of its competitiveness;
– provision of national interests and security of Russia;
– increase of Russia's share in the global trade.

Tasks in foreign trade sphere:
– provision of growth of volumes of foreign trade cooperation with China;
– change of commodity structure of Russian-Chinese foreign trade;

Possible threats for deepening of Russian-Chinese trade and economic cooperation:
– preservation of commodity structure of Russian-Chinese foreign trade;
– increase of volumes of export of raw materials to China without processing them;
– creation of processing productions in China with the use of raw materials resources of Siberia and Far East;
– formation of independence of export of raw materials from China;
– tough exploitation of Russian agricultural land for organization of export of agricultural products;
– formation of technological and financial dependence on China;
– realization of the Eurasian Land Bridge infrastructural project which bypasses Russia;
– copying Russian technologies and competition in the global markets with Russian products;

Tasks in the sphere of economic development:
– modernization of existing Russian processing industrial enterprises for increase of the processing depth of exported raw materials resources, including with attraction of foreign investments from China;
– attraction of financial resources, technologies, and highly qualified specialists for realization of large joint infrastructural projects in the sphere of extraction and processing of natural resources of Siberia and Russian Far East;
– development of transport infrastructure.

Measures of state regulation and cooperation aimed at realization of economic interests of Russia in foreign economic cooperation with China
– creation of free trade areas and joint Russian-Chinese innovational clusters for the directions that will allow obtaining multiplicative effect for Russian industry;
– support for Russian manufacturers for means of subsidizing, tax stimulation, provision of state purchases, strict technical standards for the imported products, etc.
– provision of technological superiority of Russian military complex;
– expansion of interaction in the sphere of conduct of joint scientific & technical and experimental & industrial developments;
– organization of effective control over preservation of sanitary and ecological norms in agriculture with provision of agricultural lands for rent;
– attraction of foreign workforce only on the temporary basis according to the issued quotas and organization of effective migration and transborder control;
– improvement of laws for the purpose of reduction of barriers for foreign economic activities for Russian and foreign participants in FEA;
– expansion of mutually profitable cooperation of Russia with other countries of the Asia-Pacific Region.

Fig. 5.4 Measures of state regulation and support for realization of economic interests in Russia with regard to deepening of foreign trade cooperation with China. Compiled by the authors

objects but reduces their cost), in order to reduce imports of Chinese products and support their production in Russia, with the use of Russian technologies and production base and, probably, involvement of Chinese investment. Increasing requirements related to the quality of products, Russia therefore protects the interests of its consumers and domestic manufacturers, who, increasing their volumes of production, might reduce prices in future. An example of a successful policy that protects domestic production and creates assembly production in Russia is the increase in custom taxes for used imported cars.

Therefore, it is possible to draw the following conclusions.

Firstly, China managed to achieve significant results in the global economy as a result of stage-by-stage liberalization, regulated by the state, where the policy of export expansion and active import substitution was supported by on a strategic, normative, and legal basis; the full mobilization of all types of domestic resources, including human potential; a fundamental restructuring of the economy, aimed at transition in domestic production from labour intensive products to capital and science intensive products; the attraction of foreign capital; the creation of FEAs, with their further transformation into areas of development of new and high technologies; and the policy of reducing the yuan rate.

Secondly, during the selection and realization of various joint investment projects of cluster development and the deepening of cooperation with China, it is necessary to take into consideration possible threats to the economic interests of Russia. In this regard, it is necessary to make efforts towards creating a complex of measures for state regulation and support of foreign trade cooperation between Russia and China.

Thirdly, despite that fact that China is the most suitable partner for the deepening of foreign trade relations, Russia, within its strategy to "turn to the East", should develop cooperation with other countries in the Asian-Pacific Region as well as India, as prevailing Russian–Chinese relations are unequal, and might lead to Russia's dependence on China's foreign policy. Possible threats related to a deepening of Russian–Chinese interaction should be minimized through various controls and regulations at state level.

5.3 Directions of Change of Raw Materials Vector of the Development of the Economy of the Siberian Federal District and Irkutsk Oblast in Relation to the Development of Foreign Trade Relations between Russia and China

The modern theory about clustering an economy does not connect quantity and effectiveness of created structures to the form of state structure in a certain state, the area in which it is set, or its resource base. There are many examples of unitary and

5.3 Directions of Change of Raw Materials Vector of the Development of the... 103

federative states, large and small states, and states with substantial natural resources or none at all in which created clusters modernized the national economy, the following taking place:

- Stimulated development of the living standards of the population of the country and an increase in its competitiveness;
- Changed structure of foreign trade towards growth in the share of products with a high level of processing.

We consider that in Russia's case, the federal nature of the state, its large territory, and its very rich resources base are the factors that have to become the initial reasons for transformation of its economy towards clustering. At the present stage, it is difficult to say which clusters should be given high priority, whether internal or transborder. However, it is obvious that the main role should be taken by regional authorities, which have the fullest information on sectorial development of their territory (both pros and cons); have a certain authority in law-making; can and should stimulate the formation of a business environment that corresponds to modern conditions; and, most importantly, depend on the export of their region's specialization in order to increase regional and sectorial competitiveness. Regarding the Siberian Federal District and Irkutsk Oblast, for example, analysis has shown that the economic development of the territory depends largely on the export of natural resources and the import of final products from China, the region's leading foreign trade partner.

There is an opinion that clusters are something new for Russia's economy, meaning that we do not have any experience of their development or how they work. We consider this to be a mistake. Back in the USSR, territorial and production complexes (TPCs) were developed very successfully: these were associations of economically interconnected and geographically proximate production with common infrastructure, personnel base, energy capacities, and so on (Table 5.10).

Another point is that TPCs which actively developed before the 1990s were not related to scientific research, nor aimed at the manufacture of innovational products; in addition they didn't have a competitive environment. Even the processing industries (machine building, metal processing, electric energy, manufacture of construction materials, food, and light industry) had a servicing role in the Soviet TPCs. Their activities were mainly related to development of the resource base of the country, and the improvement of the system of management and planning for complex economic and social development.

Under modern conditions, Russia should not forget its past and borrow only from the experience of foreign states in the process of clustering its economy. It is possible to created improved structures on the basis of the previously created TPCs.

Statistics shows that most of TPC were created after the 1940s in the Siberian Federal District (thanks to its unique resource base). Thus, it would be wise to emphasize the development of processing industry with a deep level of processing of raw materials in this region; in other words, to create industrial and agro-industrial clusters (Fig. 5.5).

Table 5.10 Examples of TPCs functioning in the USSR

TPC	Specialization	Correspondence to modern location
Kursk Magnetic Anomaly	Iron ore	Central FD, Russia
Timan-Pechora	Forest, mineral, and fuel and energy resources (oil, gas, and coal)	North-Western FD, Russia
Orenburg	Gas	Volga FD, Russia
Middle-Ob	Oil, gas	Ural FD, Russia
West-Siberian	Oil, gas, timber	Ural and Siberian FD, Russia
Kuzbass	Coal, production of non-ferrous metals	Siberian FD, Russia
Central-Krasnoyarsk	Coal, hydropower resources, production of non-ferrous metals, chemical production, cellulose and paper industry	
Sayansk	Fuel and energy (oil, gas, and coal) resources, iron ores, non-ferrous metals (molybdenum, gold, copper, lead, tungsten, silver), deposits of salt and construction materials (sands, clays, gravel, asbestos, gypsum, marble, granite), hydropower resources	
Irkutsk-Cheremkhovo	Coal, hydropower resources, production of non-ferrous metals, chemical production, cellulose and paper industry	
Bratsk—Ust-Ilimsk	Hydropower resources, forest resources, coal ores	Siberian FD, Russia
Norilsk	Copper-nickel ores	
Kuznetsk-Altai	Coal, non-ferrous and ferrous metal ores, chemical industry	
South-Yakutsk	Coal, iron ores, apatites, mica, nonferrous metals	Far Eastern FD, Russia
Nizhnekamsk	Raw hydrocarbon deposits, fuel and energy deposits, highly qualified personnel, developed construction base, good water supplies	Volga FD, Russia
Pavlodar-Ekibastuzsk	Coal and brown coal, sodium salt, copper	Kazakhstan
Karatau-Dzhambulsk	Phosphorites	
Mangyshlak	Oil, gas, brown coal, black-iron ore, phosphorites	
South-Tajik	Hydropower resources, sodium salt, limestone	Tajikistan

Note: compiled by the authors on the basis of the sources: Polterovich (1998), Пертцик (1984)

On the one hand, it is obvious that moving towards post-industrialization of the economy, Russia should increase service industries—primarily, those related to serving people (education, science, healthcare, etc.). However, on the other hand, it is impossible to forget the value of industry for the economy. An industry that works according to the principle "imported raw materials—exported complex (preferably science intensive) products" creates jobs, increases the population's

5.3 Directions of Change of Raw Materials Vector of the Development of the...

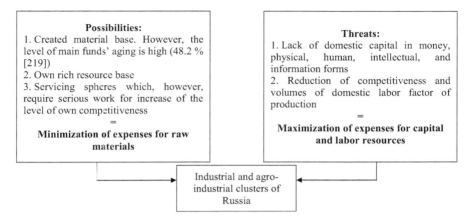

Fig. 5.5 Possibilities and threats of development of Russian industrial and agro-industrial clusters on the basis of TPCs in the Siberian Federal District. *Note*: compiled by the authors on the basis of the sources (http://expert.ru/south/2014/17/myi-mogli-poteryat-agrariev/?n=171)

well-being, forms offers and effective demand; increases the level of competitiveness at all levels of economic analysis; stimulates the growth of national wealth; guarantees national economic security; and increases the possibility that the state will receive global income as a result of the conduct of foreign trade operations, which are profitable for the country as a whole. In view of the fact that Russia has a lot of resources that are necessary for the manufacture of products with a high level of processing, its expenses for purchase of raw materials (by reducing imports to the minimum) might and should be minimized. Unfortunately, an exception is capital, which should be attracted by the state from abroad—owing to its insufficiency and low competitiveness. Here we speak not just of money, but also physical, human, intellectual, and information forms of capital. Besides, Russia should pay close attention to development of its own labour resources which, firstly, could be characterized as insufficiently competitive and, secondly, are presented in a volume that is insufficient for an industrial market. We consider that regarding the clusters created on the territory of the Siberian Federal District, support—in the form of capital and labour resources—should be sought from China, which is directly interested in access to the complex science intensive products in corresponding spheres and acquisition of technologies for their production.

It should be noted that the idea offered here is not innovative. Within national and regional economic development, a range of programmes is offered for its realization. However, these programmes are still not oriented to the creation of high-tech products but continue to be related to the deeper processing of raw materials.

For example, regional management has attempted to increase the amount of timber processing in such regions of the Siberian Federal District as Irkutsk Oblast, the Republic of Buryatia, Krasnoyarsk Krai, and Zabaykalsky Krai, where these timber products are the main article of export.

Table 5.11 Comparison of timber resources and volume of export of forestry products of Russia and Finland, 2014

Indicator	Russia in whole	Irkutsk Oblast	Finland
Total volume of export, $ billion	497.8	7.1	105.0
Cost of export of timber products, $ billion	8.4	2.7	15.0
Share of world timber resources, %	25.0	2.0	0.5
Share of global export of paper products, %	2.0	–	22.0

Note: compiled by the authors on the basis of the sources (http://www.webcitation.org; http://www.fao.org; http://www.stu.customs.ru; http://www.gks.ru; http://www.ved.gov.ru)

It has been calculated that with the largest timber resources in the world (22 % of the world stock), Russia's share in global volume of the final products of timber (cellulose, paper, cardboard, furniture, etc.) is very low—less than 2 % (Table 5.11). The volume of processed timber is also very low.

Let us note that in Finland—where forestry clusters have been functioning for a long time—despite the fact that Finland's forest resources are at least 50 times smaller than Russia's, the country's share in the global export of paper products is 11 times greater than Russia's. Using Finland's experience would allow Russia to better organize the export of forestry products.

In addition, other economic effects that might be expected from full processing of forestry products could be used within a cluster. According to our estimates, using effectiveness coefficients and offered by a range of Russian authors (Винокуров 2008, 2009) and the data of the Siberian Customs Department,[10] if all unprocessed timber exported outside Irkutsk Oblast were processed within the region, then:

– Potential value of exported timber products could increase from $2.3 billion to $180.0 billion:
– Processing of round timber into lumber log to $2.3 billion, cardboard to $6.3 billion, plywood to $7.2 billion, paper products and cellulose to $9.9 billion, furniture to $18.0 billion, and products of biological and chemical processing of timber from $90.0 billion to $180.0 billion (Table 5.12).

Thus, the fact that Russia could benefit from an increase in the depth of timber processing within a cluster is obvious; the figures show that it is much more effective to export products received during timber processing than to export round timber and lumber. Increase in the export of unprocessed timber, which brings profit only to exporters, is not beneficial either.

Currently, the Chinese are interested in the export of Russian timber and timber products, which is because they are striving to expand their circle of suppliers. Therefore, China is increasing the import of round timber from Russia, performing deep processing on Chinese territory. In 2014, $2.7 billion worth of timber products

---

[10] According to them, $1.8 billion worth of timber was exported beyond the limits of Irkutsk Oblast in 2014 (12.6 million m^3) (http://www.stu.customs.ru).

Table 5.12 Increase in the cost of timber processing products depending on processing depth

Products of timber processing	Coefficient effectiveness of processing	Cost of timber processing products, $ billion
Round timber	1.0	1.8
Lumber log	1.3	2.3
Cardboard	3.5	6.3
Plywood	4.0	7.2
Paper products and cellulose	5.5	9.9
Furniture	10.0	18.0
Products manufactured during biological or chemical processing	50–100.0	90.0–180.0

Note: compiled by the authors on the basis of the sources (Винокуров 2008)

were exported from Irkutsk Oblast to China. The capacity for processing 20–22 million m^3 of round timber purchased by China in the Siberian and Far Eastern Federal Districts is located in Manchuria, along the border with Russia. Russian timber is processed in China, and the products are exported—including to Russia (http://www.crc.mofcom.gov.cn/crweb/rcc/info/Article.jsp?col_no=107&a_no=237022).

It would be wise to attract China with its investments and production capacities to Russia, where it could manufacture—within the timber cluster—timber products that need considerable processing. These could be exported, including into China.

Beginning in 2005, investments from China into the countries of the EU constituted $87.5 billion, the USA $64.4 billion, Australia 59.6 billion, Canada $37.8 billion, Brazil $31.0 billion, Indonesia $30.0 billion, Pakistan $21.8 billion, Nigeria $20.7 billion, Saudi Arabia $18.2 billion, and Russia $17.5 billion. The oil and gas sector accounted for 26.2 % of Chinese investments, transport infrastructure and construction 21.6 %, electric energy 17.9 %, ore mining and the smelting and coal industry 15.6 %, agriculture 3.4 %, car industry 2.0 %, and other industries 13.3 % (http://www.chinapro.ru/rubrics/12/6761).

As has been seen, China is primarily interested in raw materials and the energy and transport spheres. To emphasize this, Chinese investments in Australia were aimed at the extraction and processing of metals, in Saudi Arabia at the development of the chemical industry, and in Khabarovsk Krai to complete the Amazar cellulose plant. Chinese investors conduct a rather pragmatic policy that is aimed at the receipt of profits, but with support from the state they can aim at receipt of various strategic advantages. Therefore, certain investment deals in several countries were not approved at governmental level—owing to a possible strengthening of competition from China, the outflow of technologies, or a loss of control over natural resources.

This shows that the selection and realization of joint Russian–Chinese investment projects should be conducted on the basis of Russia's national interests and provision of its economic security under state control with the application of measures and mechanisms that are aimed at developing production on Russian soil and preventing the illegal transfer of technologies or control of natural resources.

As a result, the diversification of products created by a timber processing cluster will stimulate financial stability in the region and increase revenues at all levels as well as export revenue. Developing equipment for timber processing at Russian enterprises by the Chinese will stimulate the development of a machine building complex. The use of timber processing waste (wood pellets) for heat and electricity will allow expenses to be reduced, thus increasing products' competitiveness.

Another raw material that is extracted in Russia, and could be further processed, is natural gas.

According to some estimates, Russia's share in global resources of natural gas is 25 %, and potential resources could constitute up to 40 %. The Siberian Federal District accounts for 14.0 % of initial total resources of gas, and Irkutsk Oblast for up to 4.0 %.

According to the estimates, presented in the "Strategy of development of fuel and energy complex of Irkutsk Oblast", the region's need for natural gas at the initial stage of gasification will constitute 1.5–2.5 billion m^3 per year. During the creation of gas-distributing infrastructure for supplying gas to new consumers, this will reach 4.0–6.0 billion m^3 per year. The maximum need of the region for natural gas has been assessed as 20.0–25.0 billion m^3 (Bozkurt et al. 2015). However, Irkutsk Oblast possesses significant resources of coal and hydro resources, which limit the application of natural gas as the territory's fuel. Therefore, natural gas is a potential resource for the development of gas and chemical products as technological raw materials.

It should be noted that gas from the deposits of East Siberia as a whole and Irkutsk Oblast in particular has many components, mainly methane (80 %–90 %), with a high share of ethane (up to 6 %) and helium (up to 0.4 %), and an average share of propane (2 %) and butane (1 %). A high share of these components makes the gas useful not so much as fuel but as raw materials for the development of the chemical and helium industries. The content of hydrocarbons C_2+ in the natural gas in the East Siberia deposits allows economically effective processing of natural gas within the region's gas cluster.

Simple calculations show that the economic effect from the creation of such a structure could be significant.

Firstly, it implies an increase in income from production, and further money therefore flows into budgets at various levels. Global prices for products of the first division of gas (ethane, propane, butanes) are double those of gas raw materials. Further processing of gas (etherin, propylene, butylene, etc.) quadruples the difference in cost, and the price for chemical products (spirits, glycols, etc.) is eight to ten times higher.

Secondly, another economic effect from the creation of a gas cluster could be the possibility of expanding the number of manufactured products. Gelium from gas deposits in East Siberia can be used in low-temperature division, as gelium is evolved at the end of the technological process that uses a minimum temperature. This means that the region's gas can provide all its components within one technological process.

Thirdly, an obvious economic effect is the improvement in the quality of the environment in the region and in the country, through the reduction of emissions into the atmosphere because of the transition from oil products to gas products.

Creation of a gas cluster for deep processing of raw materials in Irkutsk Oblast is encouraged by the fact that the region already possesses the necessary basis for the development of gas and chemical production. Irkutsk Oblast has a powerful oil and chemical complex which includes Sayanskkhimplast OJSC and ANKK OJSC, and these are located close to the Kovykta gas condensate field.

The need of Sayanskkhimplast OJSC for raw materials for pyrolysis (ethane and propane-butane) is up to 973.0 million m^3 per year. To obtain this, it is necessary to process 5.5 billion m^3 of natural gas per year at Sayanskkhimplast OJSC. The methane received could be used as fuel and technological raw materials at ANKK OJSC (up to 3.9 billion m^3 per year) (Alberti et al. 2014; Bozkurt et al. 2015; Caporale and Spagnolo 2012; Carneiro et al. 2015; Санеев 2010).

It should be noted that methane is the main industrial raw material for the production of hydrogen, which is the basis for the synthesis of ammonia, mineral fertilizers, azotic acid, dyes, various explosive materials, and methanol. Oxidation of the latter creates formalin, which is further used in production of plastics, tars, and paint and varnish items. In addition, methanol is used in the production of acetylene, higher alcohol, acetic acid, high-octane additives to motor oil, and bio-fuels. It is also a basic raw material for the production of technical carbomium—soot, which is used in the production of car tyres and various rubber items.

In their turn, propane, butanes, and pentans, created from natural gas, are raw materials for polymerization, and helium is used—owing to its unique attributes—in the space industry, energy, medicine, aviation, ship building, chemical and food industry, metallurgy, welding production, laser equipment, chromatography, and fundamental and applied scientific research. It cannot be replaced by any other gas or material in a range of technologies. It is a valuable non-recoverable natural resource, on the list of strategic resources—and its stock is limited.

Currently, Irkutsk Oblast has 12 % of known reserves and 63 % of Russian reserves of helium. This noble gas is present in almost all gas deposits, and its concentration in natural gas is 0.17 %–0.36 %, which is significantly higher than in regions with operating helium plants (Alberti et al. 2014; Винокуров 2009).

It seems that with the start of the full-scale extraction of gas in East Siberia, the region should have a new large helium production at federal level—moreover, a gradual depletion of helium-containing natural gas is taking place in the USA, the Netherlands, and Poland. At the same time, reserves in Qatar, Algeria, and Russia have increased (the latter because new gas deposits have been found in East Siberia). Russia may become the largest world exporter of gelium—primarily, to potential and dynamically developing markets in the Asia-Pacific Region.

At the time of writing, there is preparation under way to start the industrial development of the Chayanda field and Kovykta gas condensate field to allow exports to China and the Asia-Pacific Region of 30–40 billion m^3 of natural gas per year (Table 5.13).

Table 5.13 Expected supplies of Russian gas into the countries of the Asia-Pacific Region in 2010–2030, million m^3 per year (average values)

Supply route	2010	2015	2020	2025	2030
From West Siberia	*0*	*13*	*30*	*40*	*40*
Altai pipeline					
China	0	3	20	30	30
Gas pipeline unified system of gas supply—East Siberia—Far East (including branches to China, Korea, plants, and terminals of LNG)					
China	0	5	5	5	5
Japan	0	2	2	2	2
Korea	0	2	2	2	2
Other countries of Asia-Pacific Region	0	1	1	1	1
Total from West Siberia through the pipeline USGS—Far East	0	10	10	10	10
From East Siberia	*0*	*50*	*92*	*106*	*112*
Gas pipeline East Siberia—Far East (including branches to China, Korea, plants and terminals of LNG)					
China	0	25	55	69	75
Japan	0	5	7	7	7
Korea	0	15	20	20	20
Other countries of Asia-Pacific Region	0	5	10	10	10
Total from West Siberia through the gas pipeline West Siberia—Far East	0	50	92	106	112
From Far East (Sakhalin, Kamchatka)	13.7	21.5	38.6	53.2	57.9
From the LNG terminal in Progorodnoe and sea platforms					
China	1.4	1.8	3.0	3.8	4.0
Japan	8.2	10.8	14.0	14.6	15.0
Korea	2.7	3.6	5.2	5.9	6.0
Other countries of Asia-Pacific Region	1.4	1.8	3.2	4.1	4.3
Total from the LNG terminal in Progorodnoe and sea platforms	13.7	18.1	25.5	28.4	29.3
Through the pipeline Sakhalin—Vladivostok—Nakhodka with branches to China, Korea, from new LNG terminals in the Far East (Primorye, Kamchatka)					
China	0.0	1.0	3.9	7.4	8.6
Japan	0.0	0.2	2.1	3.7	4.3
Korea	0.0	0.8	3.3	6.2	7.1
Other countries of Asia-Pacific Region	0.0	1.4	3.8	7.4	8.6
Total through the pipeline Sakhalin—Nakhodka with branches, from new terminals	0.0	3.4	13.1	24.8	28.6
From Russia to the Asia-Pacific Region, total	137	84.5	160.6	199.2	209.9
China	1.4	35.8	87.0	115.2	122.5
Japan	8.2	18.0	25.1	27.3	28.3
Korea	2.7	21.5	30.5	34.1	35.2
Other countries of Asian-Pacific Region	1.4	9.2	18.0	22.5	23.9

Note: compiled by the authors on the basis of the sources (http://burneft.ru/archive/issues/2009-12/1)

The natural gas of East Siberia is multi-component in its structure, which gives it special value in the development of Russia's chemical industry. Thus, acquiring gas deposits and using them only as fuel and for export supplies without extracting valuable components is very ineffective.

However, according to the ideas set out by the Russian government in its Eastern gas programme, the development of the Kovykta gas field and its further connection to Siberia, oriented towards the export of gas into the markets of the Asia-Pacific Region countries—primarily, into China—will allow gas to meet the internal needs of the country, raise the region's chemical industry to a higher level, and create new jobs. However, the programme does not indicate by what means this can happen. The creation of additional infrastructure is not envisaged in the programme, and nothing is said about the strengthening of scientific and innovational components by extracting and processing. Besides, the high content of helium and other valuable components in the region's natural gas requires complex extraction and deep processing of raw materials, which, in its turn, requires the development of modern gas processing capacities.

Irkutsk Oblast has such capacities. Slight modernization will allow for the complex processing of natural gas and the receipt of valuable raw materials which are in high demand in the global market; it will also push forward the development of organic synthesis chemistry—a high tech and science intensive sphere of industry.

Apart from the production base, the region has scientific institutions. In particular, there is the Siberian branch of the Russian Academy of Sciences (RAS), which was created in 1957 as a complex of R&D, experimental, and reproduction organizations and establishments which helped the scientific centres located in Siberia to function. Currently, it is the largest regional branch of the RAS, and accounts for 20 % of its scientific potential. Its network of scientific centres, institutes, and scientific stations encompasses almost all Siberia (http://russiasib.ru/sibirskoe-otdelenie-rossijskoj-akademii-nauk-so-ran).

We believe that the complex use of natural gas, which includes its processing and creating products with a high share of added value, is the most rational. The expediency and effectiveness of this is proved by global experience. Beginning during the oil crisis of the 1970s, the high effectiveness (economic and ecological) of natural gas and its components (methane, ethane, propane, butanes, etc.) led to the gas being used in all developed countries of the world (the USA, Canada, EU, Latin America, and countries of the Persian Gulf) as technological raw materials for the chemical industry. Nowadays, the global petrochemical sphere is unique in the growth of its share of science intensive products that are used in the manufacture of chemical products. In Russia, the petrochemical industry is unique for its preservation of the tendency to manufacture and export of products which require little processing, which is caused by a lack of modern technological equipment in the country. As a result, Russia is behind the leading countries in terms of the volumes of production and consumption of chemical products (http://www.opec.org; https://yearbook.enerdata.ru.).

It seems that for the Russian chemical industry not to be behind the global level forever, the country should develop this sphere by using a cluster type of production organization, which will help to exploit the primarily highly effective gas resources of Eastern Siberia through the use of Chinese capital. In this case, a strategically important task in developing the deep processing of raw hydrocarbon deposits will be solved by forming a gas chemical industry, which will be new for the region.

Besides the helium mentioned above, the share of which in Eastern Siberian gas is very high, the region has the necessary preconditions for increasing the production of PVC, polyethylene, polystyrene, ethylene alcohol, polypropene, and other similar products which are in demand in the global market. This is because of a high percentage of ethane in local gas, significant reserves of sodium salt, and the infrastructure that has been created.

It suffices to say that the global production of PVC is currently around 30 million tons per year (with annual growth of 5 %). The Asia-Pacific Region accounts for more than 60 %. The largest growth is observed in China, Taiwan, and India. The market in the Asia-Pacific Region, primarily China, is the largest and geographically the closest to Irkutsk Oblast. However, China is developing its own industry of organic synthesis, yet it is experiencing the lack of raw hydrocarbon deposits, which restrains the growth in production of PVC. The problem created by restriction of the raw materials is solved by using artificial gas (70 % of vinyl chloride, received during production of PVC, is obtained in China by hydrochlorination of acetylene from carbide of calcium), which leads to an increase in cost of the final products. Because of this, there is a process by which acetylene technologies are being replaced by the use of natural gas. However, China is compensating by mass import—in particular, from Russia (http://www.ved.gov.ru).

The situation may change as gas from East Siberian deposits begins to be supplied to China on a large scale. This gas is noted for its high content of ethane fractions, which will positively influence the raw materials provision for the Chinese organic synthesis industry.

China is currently actively developing its capacity for the production of chemical products. This is caused not so much by competitive advantages of the country's industry (the technological process on which it is based involves imported naphtha) as by a high level of demand for chemical products. In order to reduce transport expenses and dependency on imported products, China has built several large chemical complexes for the processing of raw materials.

If, for example, the natural gas of Irkutsk Oblast is processed in Sayansk after the organization of a cluster (together with the Chinese), this city might become the largest centre for the petrochemical industry in Russia. A technological chain will start here which will provide effective raw materials to the chemical industry of the country and manufacture the export products—in this way, export effectiveness will grow significantly (http://tcj.ru).

To bring to fruition investment projects that are aimed at increasing the depth of processing of raw materials in Siberia and the Far East of Russia, in order to create and export products with a high level of added value, it is necessary to attract financial resources and use relevant technologies and equipment. Attraction of investments is possible only through the use of borrowing from Russian and Chinese banks and investment funds (Chinese credit organizations have developed a practice by which they connect the provision of financial resources with liabilities for purchase of equipment and services from Chinese enterprises and Chinese workers), as well as assets from the Asian Bank of Infrastructural Investments and the New Bank of Development of the BRICS, which were created in order to expedite infrastructural projects in Asia and in the BRICS countries, respectively.

Thus, on the basis of Chap. 3, it is possible to conclude with the following points:

Firstly, Russia, as a country that is behind China in the level of national competitiveness, for the purpose of modernizing its economy should actively use not only its own competitive advantages but those advantages of partner countries. The areas at which effective cooperation between the two countries is possible could be joint Russian–Chinese clusters, located on Russian territory. This might allow Russia to level its weak production spots; increase national commodity competitiveness; and change the commodity structure of foreign trade operations, including with China. China would receive an additional legal source of information for technologies of production in relation to complex science intensive products; access to a scientific base of applied character; and real practical areas for the creation of its own science intensive production.

Secondly, the leading role in the process of clustering in Russia's national economy should be at regional level, where the authorities are experts in all aspects of sectorial development; they have authority in the sphere of law making; they can and should stimulate the formation of a business environment that corresponds to modern conditions; and, most important, they depend on the export of regional specialization to maintain and enhance sectorial competitiveness.

As for the Siberian Federal District and Irkutsk Oblast, as territories with a unique resource base, the creation of Russian–Chinese industrial clusters on the basis of former TPCs, in both timber and gas, are necessary.

Conclusions

Modern Russian–Chinese foreign trade relations are characterized by a certain asymmetry in and limited assortment and nomenclature of goods and services offered for mutual exchange. Although at the same stage of economic development and in a single group of developing countries, Russia and China offer each other products that are different in their levels of added value, which leads to different effects on the development of their national economies. In other words, the functions set for foreign trade in Russia and China are expressed in different volumes and quality. The paradox is that, from the point of view of the theory of trade, this situation could be easily explained, and there are ways to avoid it. However, there have been no changes for a long time.

The theory of trade belongs to those that are most elaborated. Economists from various schools of political economy do not have many different opinions on the corresponding categorical apparatus; the role of trade in the sectorial structures of gross domestic product (GDP); the possible criteria of classification and, correspondingly, types; the performed functions; or the methods of conduct of trading activities. However, the theory of trade has a range of aspects that preserve difference and sometimes have a debatable character. The theory covers the causes of conduct of trade as a whole and its international component, as well as possible ways of correcting country and commodity structures of export and import for economies which are at different levels of economic development.

Economists have been searching for the answer for the issue of the causes for conducting trade, its international component, and so on for a long time, beginning from studies of mercantilists in the seventeenth century and ending with modern views of the representatives of the theory of life cycle: "national rhomb" (a system of features that, while interacting, creates favorable or unfavorable environment for realization of potential competitive advantages of the country), hypothesis of "competing groups", etc. However, one should mention that, despite these different approaches, specialists agree that a unique function of trade—exchange—should be paid the greatest attention. Understanding it properly at the state level, but not creating the conditions for simple sales of goods and services, could influence the level of development of the national economy and increase the quality of life in the country.

If the state's economy is ready for foreign economic liberalization, it will show evidence of sustainable growth rates, competitive spheres of industrial production and developing human potential. Wisely built foreign trade activities determine the volume of manufactured products; GDP and all macro-economic indicators of the system of national accounts; the share of the received global income from export operations; and, accordingly, all further payments into budgets at various levels.

If the economy is not ready for participation in the processes of exchanging goods and services in the international markets, but is nevertheless opened to foreign trade, because of a range of reasons, this may lead to outflow of capital, growth of dependence on exports, the ousting of domestic manufacturers from their own market, increasing technological underrun of the national economy, deindustrialization of production sectors, and loss of competitiveness at almost all levels.

Such significant effects of a country's participation in international trade and economic operations indicate high levels of risk—political, commercial, liquid, credit, investment, reserve, interest, currency, and other risks. The real likelihood of such risks in foreign trade pushes participants to search for adequate regulatory tools. As a result, in the evolutionary development of international trade one can observe a significant growth in the role of supernational institutes and organizations that regulate the corresponding sphere of international economic relations, and the number of countries involved in various economic and trade organizations also increases. However, if the country's economy is not ready for foreign economic liberalization, it doesn't matter how many supernational structures the country is a member of.

The economy should be gradually prepared for the unavoidable influence of external factors relating to development. There should be a clear understanding that country limits can be broadened only when there is highly competitive domestic industrial production, the products of which are characterized by certain science intensity and high level of division (liberalization of foreign trade with lack of competitive spheres of national economy that issue high-tech (knowledge-intensive) products or perform deep processing (division) of raw materials will influence negatively the socioeconomic development of the country, and national manufacturers will not survive in competitive struggle with foreign manufacturers).

This conclusion has been long proven in practice. The best results in the organization of foreign trade contacts are achieved by the largest economies of the world: those that produce the most—and buy and sell the most. Thus, there is a logical correlation between the countries that lead in the volume of foreign trade operations and economies with the largest GDP.

Reverse interconnection is also interesting. If the volume of industrial production determines the country's level of liberalization in global markets, doesn't the state policy towards foreign trade influence its economic development? Of course it does—and statistics prove this: mostly, an increase in the rates and volumes of export and/or import is followed by an increase in living standards in the country (and vice versa).

As for Russia, the long-standing commodity structure of its foreign trade does not contribute to the development of the country's economy and even aggravates its sectorial imbalances: science-intensive services develop slowly and against the background of continuing extraction of national natural resources.

Analysis of Russia's economy today has shown that, despite a strong movement towards post-industrialization, the country is drawn towards industrial types of development. Although industrial production and agriculture are declining as a proportion of GDP, with obvious growth in the service sphere, living standards in the country depend on the effectiveness of the development of industrial production, whose products dominate national exports.

Several questions arise in this situation. If the share of industrial production in GDP is reducing, and its products determine the specialization of the country in the processes of the international division of labour, what is Russia's future in terms of foreign trade policy? Should Russia narrow its industrial production to export raw materials, which are currently in demand, and then concentrate on development of the service sphere? Should Russia try to preserve its existing volumes of industrial production by means of diversification, and search for new niches in global markets as well as determining new foreign trade partners?

We recommend the second option, as the country has all necessary preconditions to support this development.

Russia's economy is characterized by a range of advantages for development. It has a rich resource base, a high-quality scientific and technological basis for the manufacture of military products, dual-purpose products, and competitive machine-building, and also a developed transport network.

Secondly, there are significant reserves of growth in the country's economy. These include its large internal market; its use of the free trade model; existing commodity niches in the global markets; a positive trading balance and external imbalance; an insignificant (as compared with GDP) external debt; and growing international reserves.

Despite such significant potential for growth, to actually achieve new goals in foreign trade policy, related to the diversification of export products, and search for new niches in the existing global commodity markets will be very difficult. This may be due to the presence of "tight spots" in the country's economy and possible threats from outside.

Among the glaring weak spots of development in the economy of modern Russia are the low level of competitiveness in a range of processing industries (car industry, micro-electronics, nano-technology products, food, and light industry); service spheres (telecommunications, finance, tourism, construction, education, science, healthcare); and agriculture.

Possible external threats that might influence further development of the economy include the probability that Russia will be assigned the status of a raw materials state; loss of control over business within the Russian economy; a growing dependence of internal economic development on the situation in the global commodity markets; a situation in the internal market of labour resources which does not conform to the strategy for Russia's development; and uncontrolled transfer of financial assets from Russia into offshore havens.

It is our contention that Russia cannot independently move from its status as a raw materials state. It needs a strategic partner in the foreign economic sphere, which, being interested in cooperation, can stimulate an increase in the level of competitiveness of the country and its people.

Analysis of Russia's modern foreign trade partners shows that, hypothetically, this strategic partner could be China, Germany, the Netherlands, Ukraine, Italy, Belarus, Turkey, the USA, Japan, or Kazakhstan. However, in view of the goals of development for Russia's economy in the mid-term, as a country that does not want to change from a subject of the global economy into an object at the periphery of global development, it should choose an equal partner. This means that Belarus, Kazakhstan, and Ukraine are the countries with which integration should be deepened and volumes of mutual trade should be increased—for the purpose of growth in national competitiveness. However, it should be recalled that Russia is the most developed and richest state in the CIS and the Customs Union. Solving such important problems as the development of R&D and the attraction of investment into specific spheres of its national economy within the groups mentioned above will be difficult. In this case, Russia, on the basis of its national interests and priorities, the level of development of foreign economic institutes, and its position in the international economy, should activate cooperation with developing Asian countries—primarily, with China.

There are several reasons for this.

First, we should consider that Asia gives Russia a chance to "trade time" for the structural reconstruction of its economy.

Secondly, China is selected from among the Asian countries because it is an acting foreign trade partner of Russia with a growing economy and a large internal market; it is also a global leader in the production of most types of industrial products.

The Chinese should be motivated by the fact that Russia has wide experience of work and competitive advantages in a range of productions. They can jointly manufacture high-tech products which are in demand in global markets.

As for the specifics of foreign trade connections with China, it is possible to note the following.

Machine-building and professional equipment make up the bulk of China's exports. The leading imported products include raw material resources necessary for work of various spheres of industry and the products of machine-building and professional equipment. In terms of volume of imports, modern China is ranked second, after the USA.

China's leading foreign trade partners are mainly developed states and new industrial countries—Hong Kong, Japan, South Korea, Taiwan, and Germany—which indirectly shows China's capability to satisfy high-tech demand.

Today, China, on the one hand, determines the climate in the global markets for its export and import products, and, on the other hand, experiences substantial dependence on the level and quality of development of its foreign trade activities.

By means of this direction, China expands the sales market of domestic (and manufactured within transnational corporations, TNC) products; effectively attracts and uses in the country the export revenue; expands the assortment of products in the internal market; receives access to deficit resources, global achievements of science and technology; and creates new jobs in export-oriented spheres of national economy.

China has successfully developed its foreign trade activities because of the following factors.

First, a wise choice in the type of foreign trade policy followed, the preparation of a strategic, normative and legal basis for it, and creation of the conditions necessary for transformation to foreign economic activities.

Secondly, the use, as a basis for foreign economic activities, of natural and wide-ranging comparative advantages: a relatively cheap workforce and human capital, of which the Chinese economy has plenty.

Thirdly, the establishment of and rapid follow-through of a policy to create free economic areas which have attracted foreign capital and helped the restructuring of economy from the manufacture of labour-intensive products to capital- and science-intensive ones.

Fourthly, adoption of a decreased currency rate.

Any consideration of Russian–Chinese trade and an economic interrelationship between the two countries should bear in mind the following. Despite a long history of interrelations between the two countries, going back as far as 1620s, and the fact that now they are characterized by a large number of touchpoints in economic, political, social, ecological, humanitarian, and other spheres of activities, the share of Russia in foreign trade operations of China is very small, constituting only 2.3 %.

The leading articles of Russian export are still fuel and energy products; timber and items of timber; ores, slag, and ashes; non-ferrous materials; and chemical products. The commodity structure of Russian imports from China preserves its product-consumer direction. The prevailing import articles are machines and equipment, chemical products, and footwear. Though, on the whole, the dynamics of developing trade cooperation between the two countries could be characterized as positive, the fact that Russia's foreign trade specialization is constantly narrowing is cause for concern. The country sells raw materials and purchases products with a higher level of division (a part of the technological process that ends with a semifinished product that could be sent to further division or sold; as a result of a product's transfer through all divisions, a final product is obtained), which contradicts all known theories of international trade. These tendencies become even more negative against the background of the growth of a negative trade balance between Russia and China.

Yet the reality of trade today between these two countries has not appeared out of nowhere. Russia has been approaching this position stage by stage. Initially, it lost its position in the Chinese military products market and then in the iron industry products market.

In this situation, specialists offer three possible scenarios for further development of two-way trade interrelations between Russia and China: parallel economic growth of both states; quick economic growth and qualitative shifts in the national economy of China without structural shifts and adequate growth of economic potential in Russia; and a lack of significant economic growth both in China and in Russia over a rather long period of time.

Based on the present reality, the third scenario is the least probable in respect of China. Accordingly, the future development of a two-way relationship between the countries depends on Russia's efforts.

Today, the official statements of political leaders on both sides treat the development of two-way relations as mutually profitable, and view this as top priority for their external policy. This will allow the strengthening of the economic power and international competitiveness of Russia and China.

The Chinese side deems it possible to achieve these goals if the commodity structure of foreign trade between the two countries changes by means of expansion of cooperation in the spheres of high technology, space and aviation, transborder infrastructure, scientific research and production, as well as growth in the quality of trade connections between the countries and the conduct of the policy of attracting mutual investments to bring to fruition large projects of strategic value on the countries' territories.

Chinese specialists emphasize the need to pay close attention to Russia's economy: to provide implementation of various innovations; increase the attractiveness of investment activities in the economy; take up measures to prevent capital outflow; develop competitiveness in the internal market and reduce influence of the state; and conduct a well-balanced budget policy for provision of Russia's financial stability.

In turn, Russian specialists think that the Chinese factor is very important for Russia's foreign policy. The role of China in accomplishing plans for the economic development of Siberia and Far East will grow over time.

Currently, Siberia and the Far East are not leaders in terms of the volume of commodity turnover with China: the top positions belong to the Central and North-Western Districts. However, the role of the Siberian Federal District (SFD) as a whole and Siberia, represented by Irkutsk Oblast, in particular, in developing foreign trade relations between Russia and China is huge. Firstly, China is the main foreign trade partner of the territory, and, secondly, the SFD (and Irkutsk Oblast) possess a large potential for extensive development. However, in the system of international division of labour in general, and trade with China especially, enterprises in the region still participate not on the basis of created and constantly improved competitive advantages, but on the basis of comparative advantages given by nature.

The commodity structure of the SFD's and Irkutsk Oblast's foreign trade operations currently differ from the commodity structure of the country as a whole. Export is dominated by raw materials and import—by machines, equipment, transport, and chemical products.

A similar commodity structure is apparent in direct Oblast trade with China. The basis of modern export to China consists of forestry products, oil and oil products,

Conclusions 121

products of chemical industry enterprises, aluminium and items made from it, machines, iron and items made from it.

The region's imports from China have for many years included machines, the volume of which grows constantly; food and mass consumption products; raw materials for aluminium; paper and cardboard.

It is obvious that if Russia is interested in expanding and deepening its connections with China the existing commodity structure of foreign trade connections both for the region and the country should be developed.

In view of the fact that, in the modern global world, resources are internationalized and their national connections are less important, we understand that Russia has changed its foreign economic policy to use its own and Chinese advantages to expedite its national tasks: to preserve Russia as a sovereign country with a high level of national competitiveness and the maximum amount of global income.

According to World Economic Forum specialists, the following indicators in Russia's economy have positive dynamics: development of institutes; infrastructure; healthcare; primary education, higher education and professional preparation; effectiveness of commodity and financial markets; labour market; innovations and the level of complexity of factors; and a range of indicators that characterize the quality of the innovational environment. Despite the clear development of Russia's economy and an increase in the level of its national competitiveness, there are some obvious problems: aggravation of the quality of the country's innovational potential (reduction of volumes and directions of the research and their implementation into economy due to decrease of financing in the current Russian foreign economic and socioeconomic conditions negatively influences the innovational activity of economic subjects), a weak macro-economic environment, and a low level of technological preparedness.

In turn, the advantages of China's economy, which exceeds Russia in its level of national competitiveness, embrace the level of institutional development; the state of the macro-economic environment (excluding the balance of state budget and state debt); the level of development of the healthcare system and primary education; the organization of the commodity market and labour market (in terms of skill of using talents); the development of the financial market and, of course, the volumes of internal and external markets; progress in competitive advantage; the complication of the added value chain; an increase in the level of control over domestic companies and over international distribution; growth in the quality of R&D institutes; domestic companies' growing budgets for R&D; strengthening of cooperation between universities and business in R&D; an increase in the role of state purchases of leading technological products; and a growth in the quality of registered patents.

Therefore Russia, to modernize its economy, which is behind China in many aspects of national competitiveness, should not refuse to consider competitive advantages created in China. In particular, it should use the innovational potential of China in the organization of joint businesses and further commodity flows.

Accumulated global experience shows that one of the most effective tools when establishing innovative economies is clustering economies. For this reason we consider that Russia should try to create joint clusters with China on Russian territory: Russia would provide science and infrastructure, China investments, workforce, and technologies. Russia will thereby receive experience of work that moves towards the development of the national economy, as well as access to the global reproduction complex with its higher-level technologies, modern tools of management, and existing infrastructure. It might leave the consumer character of Russian import and reduce the gap between Russia and leading countries as regards the innovational capability levels of the state and its subjects. It will also receive a real chance to raise weak spheres and form new ones.

It turn, China will receive an additional and legal source of information about technologies related to the production of complex science-intensive goods; access to an applied scientific base; and the development of real and practical areas related to the creation of its own science-intensive production.

Based on the specifics of the state structure of Russia's economy, we consider that the leading role in the process of clustering the national economy should belong to regional authorities, which are expert in all aspects of sectorial development of their territory; have certain authority in law-making; can and should stimulate the formation of a business environment that corresponds to modern conditions; and, most important, depend on the export of the specialization of their region in terms of regional and sectorial competitiveness.

Moreover, it is necessary to take into account the fact that the Russian regions have mostly preserved the important basis of the former territorial and production complexes (TPC). The fact that the TPC prevailed since its creation in the 1940s on the territory of the SFD (which is caused by its unique resource base) is highly significant. Therefore, it would be wise to rely on Russian–Chinese cooperation in developing processing industries with a long experience of raw materials processing in this region—all the more so now that China is already its leading foreign trade partner.

References

Abplanalp P (2007) Cluster development in a Chinese Province. In: Proceedings of the International Cluster Conference, Sun Yat-Sen University, Guangzhou

Al Mamun M, Sohag K (2015) Revisiting the dynamic effect of foreign direct investment on economic growth in LDCs. Int J Econ Policy Emerg Econ 8(2):97–118

Alberti FG, Giusti JD, Papa F, Pizzurno E (2014) Competitiveness policies for medical tourism clusters: government initiatives in Thailand. Int J Econ Policy Emerg Econ 7(3):281–309

Aleksandrova EN (2004) System of factors of economic growth of national economy. PhD thesis: 08.00.01. Krasnodar, pp 11–23

Anfinsen M, Jacobus S, Johnston C, Jones U, Böbel I (2014) Bangalore information technology cluster. Int J Econ Policy Emerg Econ 7(3):191–216

Aslam MMH, Azhar SM (2013) Globalisation and development: challenges for developing countries. Int J Econ Policy Emerg Econ 6(2):158–167

Benner M (2013) Cluster policy in developing countries. MPRA Paper No. 44257

Bhanumurthy NR, Singh P (2013) Financial sector development and economic growth in Indian states. Int J Econ Policy Emerg Econ 6(1):47–63

Bilorus O (2013) Global neo-convergence of transitive and transformative socio-economic systems. Econ Ann XXI 11–12(1):3–7

Bolotin B (2001) Global economy over 100 years. Glob Econ Int Relat (9):98

Bozkurt ÖG, Erdem C, Erollu I (2015) Identifying the factors affecting the economic growth of oil-producing countries. Int J Trade Glob Mark 8(2):97–111

Caporale GM, Spagnolo N (2012) Stock market, economic growth and EU accession: evidence from three CEECs. Int J Monet Econ Finance 5(2):183–191

Carneiro J, Matos N, Husted B (2015) Free markets and social inclusion: toward a common goal. J Bus Res 68(2):173–176

Chatterji A, Glaeser E, Kerr W (2013) Clusters of entrepreneurship and innovation. NBER Working Paper 19013. NBER, Cambridge, MA

Christensen T, Lämmer-Gamp T, Meier zu Köcker G (2012) Let's make a perfect cluster policy and cluster programme. Berlin/Copenhagen

Cooke P (1992) Regional innovation systems: competitive regulation in the new Europe. Geoforum 23:365–382

d'Abdelhamid Bencharif (2014) Valorisation des produits laitiers typiques de la Bekaa et Baalbeck-Hermel: diagnostic et stratégie locale. LACTIMED, E. Haddad/Marseille

Delgado M, Porter M, Stern S (2010) Clusters and entrepreneurship. J Econ Geogr 10:495–518

Delgado M, Porter M, Stern S (2012) Clusters, convergence, and economic performance. U.S. Census Bureau Center for Economic Studies Paper No. CES-WP-10-34

Drewello H (2013) Die Clusterlandschaft in der Trinationalen Metropolregion Oberrhein. Europäisches Kompetenz- und Forschungszentrum Clustermanagement, Kehl

Drezner DW (2014) The system worked: global economic governance during the great recession. World Polit 66(1):123–164

Edward (2012) The Triumph of the city. Penguin Publishing, New York, NY

Eltejaei E (2015) Oil, government's budget and economic growth in Iran. Int J Econ Policy Emerg Econ 8(3):213–228

Foray D, David PA, Hall B (2009) Smart specialization—the concept. Knowledge economists policy briefs. In: Knowledge for growth: prospects for the knowledge-based economy, No. 9. Glaeser

Galbraith JK (2015) Inequality and instability: a study of the world economy just before the great crisis. pp 1–336

Gehringer A (2014) Financial liberalization, financial development and productivity growth: An overview. Int J Monet Econ Finance 7(1):40–65

Geldes C, Felzensztein C, Turkina E, Durand A (2015) How does proximity affect interfirm marketing cooperation? A study of an agribusiness cluster. J Bus Res 68(2):263–272

Ghartey EE (2015) Causal relationship between financial development and economic growth in South Africa. Appl Econ Int Dev 15(1):125–142

Hausmann R, Hidalgo C, Bustos S, Coscia M, Chung S, Jimenez J, Simoes A, Yıldırım M (2012) The Atlas of economic complexity. Center for International Development/MIT Media Lab, Cambridge, MA

Helfer M (2006) Modularisierte Vorbereitung auf die Führungsverantwortung—Spezialausgabe zum Thema Modularisierung in der Weiterbildung. In: HR Today, Personalentwicklung

Hill TP (1977) On goods and services. Rev Income Wealth 23:315–338

Human Development Report (2014) [Электронныйресурс]. http://hdr.undp.org/en/content/human-development-report-2014

Inglesi-Lotz R, Van Eyden R, Du Toit C (2014) The evolution and contribution of technological progress to the South African economy: growth accounting and Kalman filter application. Appl Econ Int Dev 14(1):175–188

Inozemtsev VL (2000) Limits of overcoming development, Economic problems at the brink of ages. Ekonomika, Moscow, p 295

Inozemtsev VL (2001) Technological progress as a fundamental basis of social polarization/Megatrends of the global development. Ekonomika, Moscow, pp 26–58

Isabel D (2015) The common good model: a proposal for a global political, economic and social system. Change Manag 14(1):15–23

Jahfer A, Inoue T (2014) Financial development, foreign direct investment and economic growth in Sri Lanka. Int J Econ Policy Emerg Econ 7(1):77–93

Ketels C (2013) Cluster policy: a guide to the state of the debate. In: Knowledge and economy. Springer, Heidelberg

Klinov VG (2015) The evolution of long waves in the world economy. Stud Russ Econ Dev 26(3):285–294

Knyazeva EN (1998) Complex systems and non-linear dynamics in nature and society. Issues Philos (4):140

Knyazeva EN, Kurdyumov SP (1997) Anthropic principle in synergetics. Issues Philos (3):62

Kokodey TA (2013) History of the global business environment in the polycyclic conceptual framework. Appl Econ Int Dev 13(2):1–14

Kollontay V (2003) Western concepts of economic globalization. In: Gorbachev MS et al (eds) Aspects of globalization: difficult issues of modern development. Albina Publisher, Moscow, p 592

Ma W, Ma W (2000) Guangrong yiu mengxiang. Zhonguo: xia yige ushi nian (Слава и мечты. Китай в следующие 50 лет/ Ма Вейган и Ма Вейцзе). - Haikou: Nanhaichubanshe. – P. 72–79

Maddison A (2001) The world economy: a millennial perspective. Development Centre of the Organization for Economic Co-operation and Development, Paris

Maswana J-C, Farooki M (2013) African economic growth prospects: a resource curse perspective. Appl Econ Int Dev 13(2):173–190

Mihajlović I (2014) Possibilities for development of business cluster network between SMEs from Visegrad countries and Serbia. Serbian J Manag 9(2):145–148

Myrdal G (1996) Asian drama: an inquiry into the poverty of nations. Pantheon, New York, NY, p 189 (стр.18)

Nikolaeva IP, Shakhovskaya LS, Popkova EG et al (2004) Economic theory. In: Nikolaeva IP (ed) Transforming economy: study guide. UNITI-DANA, Moscow

Othman J, Jafari Y, Sarmidi T (2014) Economic growth, foreign direct investment, macroeconomic conditions and sustainability in Malaysia. Appl Econ Int Dev 14(1):213–223

Polterovich VM (1998) Institutional traps and economic reforms. RES, Moscow

Popkova EG (2010a) "Underdevelopment whirlpools" as instrument of world economy polarization measurement. In: Popkova EG, Shakhovskaya LS, Mitrakhovich TN (eds). Glob Bus Econ Anthol I:304–309

Popkova EG (2010b) Disproportions of economic growth in regions of the RF: problems of analysis. In: Popkova EG, Mitrakhovich TN (eds). Mod Econ Probl Solut (2):24–36

Popkova EG (2010c) Instrumentarium of analysis of disproportions of economic growth. In: Popkova EG, Mitrakhovich TN (eds). Russian economy: from crisis to modernization: materials of international scientific and practical conference (Sochi, January 28–30, 2010), vol 3. Kuban State University et al., Krasnodar, pp 52–53

Popkova EG (2011) "Underdevelopment whirlpools" as a tool of spatial and temporal measurement of economic development. In: Popkova EG, Mitrakhovich TN (eds). J Int Sci Publ Econ Bus 5(Part 1):298–306

Popkova EG (2013) Marketing strategy to overcome the "underdevelopment whirlpool" of the Volgograd region. In: 11th EBES Conference. Ekaterinburg (Ekaterinburg, Russia, September 12–14, 2013): Proceedings. The Institute of Economics Ural Branch of Russian Academy of Sciences, Istanbul, Turkey, pp 52–61

Popkova E (2014) New prospects of economic growth in context of underdevelopment whirlpools phenomena. Appl Econ Int Dev 14(1):5–25

Popkova EG, Tinyakova VI (2013a) New quality of economic growth at the present stage of development of the world economy. World Appl Sci J 24(5):617–622

Popkova EG, Tinyakova VI (2013b) Drivers and contradictions of formation of new quality of economic growth. Middle East J Sci Res 11:1635–1640

Popkova EG, Tinyakova VI (2013c) Drivers and contradictions of formation of new quality of economic growth. Middle East J Sci Res 15(11):1635–1640

Popkova EG, Tinyakova VI (2013d) Dialectical methodology of analysis of economic growth. World Appl Sci J 24(4):467–475

Popkova EG, Zubakova NN, Bogdanov DV, Yakovleva EA, Nebesnay AY (2013a) Measurement of economic growth as a factor of development of strategies of economic transformation. World Appl Sci J 25(2):264–269

Popkova EG, Dubova UI, Romaniva MK (2013b) Designing the territorial marketing strategy on the principles of cluster policies. World Appl Sci J 22(4):571–576

Popkova EG, Morkovina SS, Patsyuk EV, Panyavina EA, Popov EV (2013c) Marketing strategy of overcoming of lag in development of economic systems. World Appl Sci J 56(5):591–595

Popkova EG, Akopova ES, Budanova IM, Natsubidze AS (2013d) The directions of transition of economic systems to new quality of economic growth. World Appl Sci J 26(9):1180–1184

Popkova EG, Yurev V, Stepicheva O, Denisov N (2015) Transformation and concentration of intellectual capital as a factor of economic growth in the modern economy. Reg Sect Econ Stud 15(1):53–60

Pulselli FM, Coscieme L, Neri L, Regoli A, Sutton PC, Lemmi A, Bastianoni S (2015) The world economy in a cube: a more rational structural representation of sustainability. Glob Environ Chang 35:41–51

Qoboa M, Dubeb M (2015) South Africa's foreign economic strategies in a changing global system. South Afr J Int Aff 22(2):145–164

Reveiu A, Dârdală M (2015) Influence of cluster type business agglomerations for development of entrepreneurial activities study about Romania. Amfiteatru Econ 17(38):107–119

Roy X, Lee C-H, Crowther AC, Schenck CL, Besara T, Lalancette RA, Siegrist T, Stephens PW, Brus LE, Kim P, Steigerwald ML, Nuckolls C (2013) Nanoscale atoms in solid-state chemistry. Science. doi:10.1126/science.1236259

Savic N, Pitic G, Konjikusic S (2014) Microeconomic and macroeconomic determinants of competitiveness of East European countries in 2012. Int J Econ Policy Emerg Econ 7(3):264–280

Schumpeter J (1982) The theory of economic development: an inquiry into profits, capital, credit, interest, and the business cycle. Progress, Moscow, pp 159–169

Scott AJ (2012) A World in emergence: cities and regions in the 21st century. Edward Elgar Publishers, Cheltenham

Shakhovskaya LS (2006) New prospects of economic growth: modern vision paradigm. In: Shakhovskaya LS, Popkova EG (eds). Glob Bus Econ Anthol I:428–439

Škare M, Sinković D (2013) The role of equipment investments in economic growth: a cointegration analysis. Int J Econ Policy Emerg Econ 6(1):29–46

Sukharev O (2003) Modern concepts of economic development. Ekonomist (7):30–45 (p 35)

Teekasap P (2014) Intellectual property rights and productivity growth from technology spillover in Thailand: a system dynamics approach. Int J Econ Policy Emerg Econ 7(4):366–382

Timofeev IS (1972) Methodological purpose of the categories "quality" and "quantity". Nauka, Moscow

Wamboye E, Adekola A (2013) Can small and medium multinational enterprises offer an alternative to multinational corporations in African countries? Evidence from Nigeria. Int J Econ Policy Emerg Econ 6(3):279–295

World Bank (2013) Clusters for competitiveness, international trade department. World Bank, Washington, DC

Xavier Molina-Morales F, Belso-Martínez JA, Más-Verdú F, Martínez-Cháfer L (2015) Formation and dissolution of inter-firm linkages in lengthy and stable networks in clusters. J Bus Res 68(7):1557–1562

Официальный сайт Всемирного банка [Электронный ресурс]. http://www.worldbnk.org

Официальный сайт Всемирной торговой организации [Электронный ресурс]. http://www.wto.int

Официальный сайт газеты «Жэньминь жибао» онлайн на русском языке [Электронный ресурс]. http://russian.people.com.cn/31519/8180469.html

Официальный сайт Конференции ООН по торговле и развитию (ЮНКТАД) [Электронный ресурс]. www.unctad.org/fdistatistics

Официальный сайт Международного радио Китая [Электронный ресурс]. http://russian.cri.cn

Прогноз развития мировой торговли HSBC [Электронный ресурс]. http://www.hsbc.ru/1/PA_1_1_S5/content/russia/about_us/news/pdf/rus/Press_release_Global_trade_forecast_from_HSBC_RUS_11_10_2011.pdf

Рейтинг 500 крупнейших мировых компаний [Электронный ресурс]. http://money.cnn.com/magazines/fortune/global500/2012/full_list/

Доклад секретариата Конференции ООН по торговле и развитию. Нью-Йорк, ООН, 1987. С. 193

Всемирный экономический форум: Рейтинг стран мира по уровню конкурентоспособности путешествий и туризма в 2015 году. [Электронный ресурс] // Центр гуманитарных технологий. – 2015.05.07. http://gtmarket.ru/news/2015/05/07/7152

Изменение доли ОАО «РЖД» на рынке транспортных услуг. Официальный сайт ОАО «РЖД» [Электронный ресурс]. http://annrep.rzd.ru/reports/public/ru?STRUCTURE_ID=4389&

References

Индекс сетевой готовности. Гуманитарная энциклопедия [Электронный ресурс] // Центр гуманитарных технологий. – 2009.10.25 (последняя редакция: 2015.04.17). http://gtmarket.ru/ratings/networked-readiness-index/networked-readiness-index-info

Официальный сайт «World Economic Journal» [Электронный ресурс]. http://world-economic.com/ru/articles_wej-350.html

Официальный сайт Всемирного банка [Электронный ресурс]. http://www.worldbnk.org

Официальный сайт Всемирной организации здравоохранения [Электронный ресурс]. http://apps.who.int/gho/data/node.main.75?lang=en

Официальный сайт Всемирной торговой организации [Электронный ресурс]. http://www.wto.int

Официальный сайт журнала «Эксперт» [Электронный ресурс]. http://expert.ru/south/2014/17/myi-mogli-poteryat-agrariev/?n=171

Официальный сайт Информационного агентства «REGNUM» http://www.regnum.ru/news/polit/1898196.html#ixzz3SfMpVAn0

Официальный сайт Китайского информационного Интернет-центра [Электронный ресурс]. http://russian.china.org.cn/

Официальный сайт министерства сельского хозяйства Российской Федерации [Электронный ресурс]. http://www.mcx.ru

Официальный сайт Министерства экономического развития Российской Федерации [Электронный ресурс]. http://www.economy.gov.ru

Официальный сайт Национального бюро статистики Китайской Народной Республики [Электронный ресурс]. http://www.stats.gov.cn

Официальный сайт Национального рейтингового агентства [Электронный ресурс]. http://www.ra-national.ru/?page=raiting-credit

Официальный сайт Организации Объединённых Наций по промышленному развитию (ЮНИДО) [Электронный ресурс]. http://www.unido.org

Официальный сайт Президента Российской Федерации [Электронный ресурс]. http://www.президент.рф

Официальный сайт Сетевого издания «РИА Новости» [Электронный ресурс]. http://www.ria.ru

Официальный сайт Стокгольмского института исследования проблем мира [Электронный ресурс]. http://www.sipri.org/databases

Официальный сайт Таможни Китайской Народной Республики [Электронный ресурс]. http://www.customs.gov.cn

Официальный сайт Федерального космического агентства [Электронный ресурс]. http://www.federalspace.ru/114

Официальный сайт Федеральной службы государственной статистики Российской Федерации [Электронный ресурс]. http://www.gks.ru

Официальный сайт Федеральной таможенной службы Российской Федерации [Электронный ресурс]. http://www.customs.ru

Официальный сайт Центрального банка Российской Федерации [Электронный ресурс]. http://www.cbr.ru.

Портал внешнеэкономической информации Министерства внешнеэкономического развития Российской Федерации [Электронный ресурс]. http://www.ved.gov.ru

Портал о российском газе [Электронный ресурс]. http://gasforum.ru/obzory-i-issledovaniya/232

Рейтинг стран мира по уровню продовольственной безопасности в 2014 году. [Электронный ресурс] // Центр гуманитарных технологий. – 2014.05.29. http://gtmarket.ru/news/2014/05/29/6788

Рейтинг стран мира по уровню развития Интернета. Гуманитарная энциклопедия [Электронный ресурс] // Центр гуманитарных технологий. – 2012.05.23 (последняя редакция: 2015.02.06). http://gtmarket.ru/ratings/internet-development/info

Рейтинг стран мира по уровню развития информационно-коммуникационных технологий. Гуманитарная энциклопедия [Электронный ресурс] // Центр гуманитарных технологий. – 2009.10.23 (последняя редакция: 2014.11.24). http://gtmarket.ru/ratings/ict-development-index/ict-development-index-info

Рейтинг стран мира по уровню развития электронного правительства. Гуманитарная энциклопедия [Электронный ресурс] // Центр гуманитарных технологий. – 2012.03.07 (последняя редакция: 2015.02.10). http://gtmarket.ru/ratings/e-government-survey/info

Рейтинг стран мира по уровню расходов на здравоохранение. Гуманитарная энциклопедия [Электронный ресурс] // Центр гуманитарных технологий. – 2012.05.22 (последняя редакция: 2015.03.26). http://gtmarket.ru/ratings/expenditure-on-health/info

Винокуров М.А. Ресурсы и запасы природного газа в Иркутской области / М.А. Винокуров // Известия ИГЭА. – 2009. – №2. – С. 24–30

Винокуров М.А. Что теряют Россия в целом и Иркутская область в частности от неэффективной работы лесопромышленного комплекса / М.А. Винокуров // Известия ИГЭА. – 2008. – №3. – С. 25–26

Ли Хуа Китайская открытая стратегия экономического развития / Хуа Ли // Журнал финансового института Юннан. – 2001, № 6. С. 35–37

Пертцик В.А. Организационно-правовые проблемы территориально-производственных комплексов / В.А. Пертцик. // Правоведение. -1984. - № 1. - С.65–75

Санеев Б.Г. Энергетика Байкальского региона как основа устойчивого развития / Б.Г. Санеев, С.Ю. Музычук // Известия ИГЭА (электронная версия). – 2010. – №4

Столярова Е.С. Внешнеэкономическая стратегия КНР в начале XXI в. и миграционная политика / Е.С.Столярова // Вестник Томского государственного университета. 2009. № 327. С. 86–89

Глобальный индекс инноваций. Гуманитарная энциклопедия [Электронный ресурс] // Центр гуманитарных технологий. – 2011.06.15 (последняя редакция: 2014.07.18). http://gtmarket.ru/ratings/global-innovation-index/info

Годовой статистический бюллетень Организации стран – экспортеров нефти [Электронный ресурс]. http://www.opec.org

Исследование INSEAD: Глобальный индекс инноваций 2014 года. [Электронный ресурс] // Центр гуманитарных технологий. – 2014.07.18. http://gtmarket.ru/news/2014/07/18/6841

Коржубаев А.Г. Перспективы развития нефтяной и газовой промышленности Сибири и Дальнего Востока и прогноз экспорта нефти и газа из России на Тихоокеанский рынок / А.Г. Коржубаев, И.А.Соколова, Л.В.Эдер // Журнала «Бурение и нефть» [Электронный ресурс]. http://burneft.ru/archive/issues/2009-12/1

Официальный сайт «Российской газеты» [Электронный ресурс]. http://www.rg.ru/2011/06/10/china.html

Официальный сайт «Химического журнала» [Электронный ресурс]. http://tcj.ru

Официальный сайт Всемирного экономического форума [Электронный ресурс]. http://www.weforum.org

Официальный сайт Всемирной туристической организации [Электронный ресурс]. http://www.webcitation.org

Официальный сайт журнала «ChinaPRO» [Электронный ресурс]. http://www.chinapro.ru/rubrics/12/6761

Официальный сайт журнала «Эксперт» [Электронный ресурс]. http://expert.ru/south/2014/17/myi-mogli-poteryat-agrariev/?n=171

Официальный сайт Международного валютного фонда [Электронный ресурс]. http://www.imf.org

Официальный сайт Министерства финансов Китайской Народной Республики [Электронный ресурс]. http://www.mof.gov.cn

Официальный сайт Продовольственной и сельскохозяйственной организации Объединенных Наций [Электронный ресурс]. http://www.fao.org

Официальный сайт Сибирского таможенного управления [Электронный ресурс]. http://www.stu.customs.ru

Официальный сайт Федеральной службы государственной статистики Российской Федерации [Электронный ресурс]. http://www.gks.ru

Официальный сайт Центра международной торговли [Электронный ресурс]. http://www.intracen.org/tradstat/welcome.htm

Портал внешнеэкономической информации Министерства внешнеэкономического развития Российской Федерации [Электронный ресурс]. http://www.ved.gov.ru

Рейтинг стран мира по уровню научно-исследовательской активности. Гуманитарная энциклопедия [Электронный ресурс] // Центр гуманитарных технологий. – 2012.05.26 (последняя редакция: 2014.07.07). http://gtmarket.ru/ratings/scientific-and-technical-activity/info

Рейтинг стран мира по уровню расходов на НИОКР. Гуманитарная энциклопедия [Электронный ресурс] // Центр гуманитарных технологий. – 2013.05.26 (последняя редакция: 2014.07.07). http://gtmarket.ru/ratings/research-and-development-expenditure/info

Российско-Китайское торгово-экономическое сотрудничество [Электронный ресурс]. http://www.crc.mofcom.gov.cn/crweb/rcc/info/Article.jsp?col_no=107&a_no=237022

Статистический Ежегодник мировой энергетики 2014 [Электронный ресурс]. https://yearbook.enerdata.ru.

Энциклопедия Сибири [Электронный ресурс]. http://russiasib.ru/sibirskoe-otdelenie-rossijskoj-akademii-nauk-so-ran

Further Reading

О заключении Соглашения между Правительством Российской Федерации и Правительством Китайской Народной Республики об инвентаризации договоров, заключенных между СССР и Китайской Народной Республикой в период с 1949 по 1991 год: Постановление Правительства РФ №166 от 12.02.1999 [электронный ресурс] // Консультант Плюс

О программе создания в Восточной Сибири и на Дальнем Востоке единой системы добычи, транспортировки газа и газоснабжения с учетом возможного экспорта газа на рынки Китая и других стран АТР: Приказ Минпромэнерго России №340 от 03.09.2007 [Электронный ресурс]. // Консультант Плюс

О ратификации договора о добрососедстве, дружбе и сотрудничестве между Российской Федерацией и Китайской Народной Республикой: Федеральный закон РФ №9-ФЗ от 25.01.2002 [Электронный ресурс] // Консультант Плюс

Об утверждении перечня инновационных территориальных кластеров: Поручение Председателя Правительства Российской Федерации №ДМ-П8-5060 от 28.08.2012 [Электронный ресурс]. // Консультант Плюс

Об основах государственного регулирования внешнеторговой деятельности: Федеральный закон РФ №164-ФЗ от 08.12.2003 [Электронный ресурс]// Консультант Плюс

Об утверждении Концепции долгосрочного социально-экономического развития Российской Федерации на период до 2020года: Распоряжение Правительства Российской Федерации №1662-р от 17.11.2008 [Электронный ресурс]. // Консультант Плюс

Об утверждении Стратегии инновационного развития РФ на период до 2020года: Распоряжение Правительства РФ №2227-р от 08.12.2011 [Электронный ресурс]. // Консультант Плюс

Об утверждении стратегии развития топливно-энергетического комплекса Иркутской области до 2015-2020 и на перспективу до 2030 года: распоряжение Правительства Иркутской области №491-рп от 12.10.2012 [Электронный ресурс] // Консультант Плюс

Об утверждении Стратегии развития химического и нефтехимического комплекса на период до 2030 года: Приказ Минпромторга России №651 и Минэнерго России №172 от 08.04.2014 [Электронный ресурс]. // Консультант Плюс

Обутверждении Стратегии развития химической и нефтехимической промышленности на период до 2015года: Приказ Минпромэнерго РФ №119 от 14.03.2008 [Электронный ресурс]. // Консультант Плюс

Обутверждении Стратегии социально-экономического развития Дальнего Востока и Байкальского региона на период до 2025года: Распоряжение Правительства РФ № 2094-р от 28.12.2009 [Электронный ресурс]. // Консультант Плюс

Обутверждении Стратегии социально-экономического развития Сибири до 2020 года: Распоряжение Правительства РФ №1120-р от 05.07.2010 [Электронный ресурс] // Консультант Плюс

Программа сотрудничества между регионами Дальнего Востока и Восточной Сибири Российской Федерации и Северо-Востока Китайской Народной Республики (2009-2018 годы) [Электронный ресурс]. http://kp.ru/upfile/attached_file/559291.doc

Монографии, диссертации, учебные пособия

Аблова Н.Е. История КВЖД и российской эмиграции в Китае (первая половина XX в.). - Мн.: БГУ, 1999. - 316 с

Авдокушин Е.Ф. Страны БРИКС в современной мировой экономике / Е.Ф. Авдокушин, М.В. Жариков. М., 2013. – 480 с

Бартенев С.А. История экономических учений: Учебник. - М.: Экономистъ, 2004. - 456 с

Богатуров А.Д. Противоречия «конкурентного сосуществования» 1956-1958гг. Тайваньский кризис (август 1958 г.). – М.: 2000.- гл. 5, с.597

Борисов А.Б. Большой экономический словарь. – М.: Книжный мир, 2003. – 895 с

Борисов О.Б., Колосков Б.Т. Советско-китайские отношения, 1945-1980 3-е изд., доп. – Москва: Мысль, 1980. – 638 с

Брагинский О.Б. Мировая нефтехимическая промышленность. М., Наука, 2003 г. - 556 с

Брюне Антуан, Гишар Жан-Поль. Геополитика меркантилизма: новый взгляд на мировую экономику и международные отношения: пер. с фр. / Гишар Жан-Поль Брюне Антуан. – М.: Новый хронограф, 2012. – 232 с

Винокуров М.А., Суходолов А.П. Экономика Сибири: 1900–1928. – «Наука». Сибирская издательская фирма РАН, 1996. – 320 с

Галенович Ю.М. Взгляд на Россию из Китая. Прошлое и настоящее России и наших отношений с Китаем в трактовке китайских ученых. М.; Время, 2010. – 304 с

Галенович Ю.М. Китайские претензии: Шесть крупных проблем в истории взаимоотношений России и Китая. М.; «СПСЛ», «Русская панорама», 2015.– 1136 с

Галенович Ю.М. От Брежнева и Мао Цзэдуна до Горбачева и Дэн Сяопина. М.; ИДВ РАН, 2012. – 224 с

Галенович Ю.М. Россия в «китайском зеркале». Трактовка в КНР в начале XXI века истории России и русско-китайских отношений. – М.: Восточная книга, 2011. – 416 с

Гельбрас В.Г. Китайская реальность России. / В.Г. Гельбрас. - М.: ИД «Муравей», 2001. – 320 с

Гельбрас В.Г. Экономика Китайской Народной Республики. Важнейшие этапы развития, 1949–2007. Курс лекций. – Москва: Гуманитарий, 2007. – 424 с

Геоэкономика и конкурентоспособность России: Научно-концептуальные основы геоэкономической политики России: Научно-аналитический доклад / М.Ю. Байдаков, Н.Ю. Конина, Э.Г. Кочетов, Е.В. Сапир, В.Л. Сельцовский, Н.С. Столярова, Е.Д. Фролова; Под науч. ред. Э.Г. Кочетова; Обществ. ак. наук геоэкономики и глобалистики. М.: Книга и бизнес, 2010. 388 с

Китайская экономика в XXI веке. Селищев А.С., Селищев Н.А. СПб.: Питер, 2004. – 240 с

Кокарев К.А. Политический режим и модернизация Китая. М.: ИДВ РАН 2004. - 320 с

Колесов В.П., Кулаков М.В. Международная экономика: К60 Учебник.- М.: ИНФРА-М, 2004. - 474 с

Крие А., Жаллэ Ж. Внутренняя торговля. Пер с фр/ Общ. ред. В.С. Загашвили. - М.: АО Издательская группа «Прогресс» - «Универс», 1993. - с

Кураков Л.П., Кураков В.Л., Кураков А.Л. Экономика и право: словарь-справочник. – Москва: Вуз и школа, 2004. – 1072 с

Ларин В.Л. Основные проблемы международных отношений в Восточной Азии в начале XXI века. Владивосток: Дальнаука, 2005. - 24 с

Ломакин В.К. Мировая экономика: Учебник для вузов. - 2-е изд., перераб. и доп. - М.: ЮНИТИ-ДАНА, 2002. - 735 с. С.420

Лоу Цзивэй. Реформы Китая: волновой период // изд. Китайского развития, – 2001. Т. 6

Лузянин С.Г. «Россия и Китай в Евразии» – М. ИД «Форум» 2009, 288 с

Лузянин С.Г. Шанхайская организация сотрудничества 2013-2015. Прогнозы, сценарии и возможности развития. М.: ИДВ РАН, 2013. 120 С

Лузянин С.Г., Гордиенко Д.В. Оценка уровня безопасности стран Северо-Восточной и Центральной Азии. М.; ИДВ РАН, 2013. – 88 с

Майоров С. Внешняя политика Советского Союза в период Отечественной войны: Документы и материалы. - М, Госполитиздат, 1946, Т.3. с. 458–461

Маркс К., Энгельс Ф. Соч. 2-е изд. Т. 26. Ч. 1. С. 413

Мастепанов А.М. Топливно-энергетический комплекс России на рубеже веков: состояние, проблемы и перспективы развития. Справочно-аналитический сборник. Т.1. М.; Издательство ИАЦ «Энергия», 2009. - 530 с

Международная торговля услугами: учеб. пособие / А.И.Лылов, А.И.Тимофеев; Воронеж. гос. ун-т. - Воронеж: Изд-во Воронеж. гос. ун-та, 2006.- 248 с

Международные экономические отношения: Учебник для вузов/ В.Е.Рыбалкин, Ю. А.Щербанин, Л.В.Балдин и др.; Под ред. проф. В.Е.Рыбалкина.- 4-е изд., перераб. и доп. - М.: ЮНИТИ-ДАНА, 2003. – 519 с

Никольский А.В. КНР. Краткий исторический очерк (1949-1979 гг.). – М.: Издательство политической литературы, 1980. – 206 с

Ожегов С.И., Шведова Н.Ю. Толковый словарь русского языка. – М., 1999. С. 476

Островский А.В. Китайская модель перехода к рыночной экономике / А.В Островский. М., 2007. - 208 с

Поздняков В.Я., Казаков С.В. Экономика отрасли Учеб. пособие. – М.: ИНФРА-М, 2010. – 309 с

Полозюкова О.Е. Особенности экономики Китая на современном этапе и перспективы ее развития: автореф. канд. эконом наук. – М., 2012. – 27 с

Попова Т.Н. Внешнеэкономическая деятельность: Учебное пособие. - Владивосток: ТИДОТ ДВГУ, 2001. - 75 с

Райзберг Б.А., Лозовский Л.Ш., Стародубцева Е.Б. Современный экономический словарь. 5-е изд., перераб. и доп. – М.: ИНФРА-М, 2007. – 495 с

Риккардо Д. Начала политической экономии и налогообложения / Д. Риккардо// Соч. – М., 1955. – Т. 1. – 360 с

Родников А.Н. Логистика: Терминологический словарь. М., 2000. С. 147

Российский энциклопедический словарь: РЭС: в 2 кн./ Гл. ред. А.М.Прохоров, редкол.: В.И. Бородулин, А.П. Горкин (Зам. гл. ред.), В.М.Карев [и др.]. – М.: Большая Рос. энцикл., 2001

Русско-китайские отношения 1689–1916. Офиц. документы. М., 1958

Русско-китайские отношения в XVII веке: Материалы и документы. М., 1969. Т. 1. 1606–1683. С. 251–252

Русско-китайские отношения. 1689-1916. Официальные документы. – М.: Издательство восточной литературы, 1958. – 138 с

Сборник договоров России с другими государствами. 1856-1917. М., Гос.изд-во полит. литературы, 1952

Сборник договоров России с Китаем. 1689-1881 гг. / Министерство иностранных дел, 1889

Серия «Деловая Франция» Анри Крие, Жоэль Жаллэ. Перевод с французского Б.П. Нарумова. Общая редакция к.э.н. В.С. Загашвили. – М. Изд. группа «прогресс» 1993. - 192 с

Сладковский М.И. Китай – основные проблемы истории, экономики, идеологии. – М.: Мысль, 1978. – 300 с

Сладковский М.И. Очерки экономических отношений СССР с Китаем. М., 1957

Смит А. «Исследование о природе и причинах богатства народов». Л.: Госсоцэкгиз, 1935. Т.2.-475 с

Современные проблемы КНР. (Аналитика ученых Университета Цинхуа). Часть 2. Экспресс-информация. Ред.- Горбунова С.А. Авт. ориг.- Ху Аньган - М.; ИДВ РАН, 2014. - 115 с

Суходолов А.П., Цвигун И.В., Павловская Т.В., Внешнеэкономическая деятельность Иркутской области в 2002 году. / Интеграция России, Сибири и дальнего Востока в систему мирохозяйственных связей: теория и практика. – Иркутск, 2003

Титаренко М.Л. Геополитическое значение Дальнего востока. Россия, Китай и другие страны Азии. – М.: Памятники исторической мысли. 2000. – 624 с

Титаренко М.Л. Международный и внутристрановой контекст формирования и развития стратегического партнерства между Россией и Китаем / М.Л. Титаренко, А.В. Виноградов // Стратегический партнерский диалог между Россией и Китаем. Современное состояние, проблемы и предложения.– М., 2014.– Кн.1.– С.11–17

Титаренко М.Л. Россия и ее азиатские партнеры в глобализирующемся мире. Стратегическое сотрудничество: проблемы и перспективы / М.Л. Титаренко. М.: ИД «ФОРУМ», 2012. - 544 с

Титаренко М.Л. Россия и Китай: стратегическое партнерство и вызовы времени / М.Л. Титаренко. – М.: ИД «ФОРУМ», 2014. – 224 с

Усов В.Н. КНР: «от большого скачка» к «культурной революции» (1960–1966гг.) ИДВ РАН. Москва, 1998

Финансовый менеджмент: Учебник для вузов Под. ред. акад. Г.Б. Поляка. – 2-е изд., перераб. и доп. – М.: ЮНИТИ-ДАНА, 2006. - 527 с

Хохлов А.В. География мирового лесопромышленного комплекса. Тула: Гриф и К, 2007. – 300 с

Цвигун И.В., Мэн Дэмин. Формирование китайских трансграничных корпораций на основе государственной стратегии «выход за границу» / И.В. Цвигун, Мэн Дэмин. - Иркутск: Изд-во БГУЭП, 2010. - 148 с

Экономическая география СССР: Учеб. для экон. спец. вузов / А.Н. Лаврищев, 382, 5-е изд., перераб. и доп. М. Экономика. 1986

Авдокушин Е.Ф. Новая экономика и формирование национальной инновационной системы Китая // Вопросы новой экономики. 2010. № 1. – С. 23–35

Авдокушин Е.Ф. О сути и особенностях китайской экономической модели // Вопросы новой экономики. 2013. №1 (25). – С.23–26

Акимова О.Е. Перспективы торгово-экономического сотрудничества России и Китая / О.Е. Акимова, В.В. Исаев // Изв. Волгогр. гос. техн. ун-та.– 2013.–№11(114).– С.51–55

Альбеков А. Инструменты государственно-частного партнерства в российской практике реализации инфраструктурных проектов / А. Альбеков, А. Кизим, А. Демченко // Логистика. 2014.– №5(90). – С. 50–54

Ань Чжао Чжэнь. Эффективный путь к всестороннему развитию экономических связей между Китаем и Россией / Ань Чжао Чжэнь, Д.В. Суслов // Власть и упр. на Востоке России.– Хабаровск, 2013.– №4.– С.14–20

Арутюнов В. Газохимия как катализатор инновационного развития России. Промышленные ведомости. 2004. №9–10 (86–87). С.1

Банников А.Ю. Оценка развития химических кластеров Германии / А.Ю. Банников // Проблемы современной экономики. – 2013. – № (47) – С. 373–377

Белоглазов Г.П. Россия и Китай в современном мире // Россия и АТР.– 2014.– №2.– С.207–212

Бирюков А.В. Опыт Китая: уроки для России // Россия: тенденции и перспективы развития.– 2013.– Вып.8, ч.1.– С.12–17

Богомолов О.Т. Сложный путь интеграции России в мировую экономику / О.Т. Богомолов // Мировая экономика и международные отношения. – 2003.– № 9. – С. 3–12

Бутаев Ф.Ф. Развитие экспорта российского природного газа в страны Азиатско-Тихоокеанского региона: геоэкономические аспекты: на примере Китая и Японии: диссертация … кандидата экономических наук: 08.00.14 / Бутаев Фируз Фаррухович. - М, 2009. - 205 с

Ведомости Верховного Совета СССР, 16 ноября 1950 г. № 36 (651), с.4

Винокуров М.А. Перспективы газификации Иркутской области / М.А. Винокуров // Известия ИГЭА. – 2009. – №3. – С. 30–33

Винокуров М.А. Предложения органам федеральной власти по совершенствованию работы некоторых отраслей / М.А. Винокуров, А.П. Суходолов // Известия ИГЭА. – 2009. – №5. – С. 5–11

Винокуров М.А. Российская экономика: необходимость модернизации и инновационного развития / М.А. Винокуров, А.П. Суходолов // Известия ИГЭА. – 2009. – №6. – С. 5–13

Гойхберг Л. Национальная инновационная система России в условиях «новой экономики» // Вопросы экономики. – 2003. – №3. – С. 30–36

Городничая Е.И. Зарубежный опыт стимулирования формирования кластеров / Е.И. Городничая // Вестник Московского университета. Сер. 6: Экономика. – 2010. – № 1. – С. 15–26

Дюмулен И.И. Внешнеэкономические связи России. Достижения и проблемы / И.И. Дюмулен // Российский внешнеэкономический вестник. 2008. – №7. – С. 21–26

Дюмулен И.И. Международная торговля 2007-2010гг.: некоторые уроки глобального экономического кризиса / И.И. Дюмулен // Российский внешнеэкономический вестник. 2010. – № 7. – С. 3–10

Елькин И.В. Влияние развития экспортного потенциала на экономику региона и рост уровня благосостояния населения / И.В. Елькин // Известия ИГЭА. – 2008. – №3. – С. 105–108

Иванов С.А. Особые экономические зоны в Китае: уроки для дальневосточной политики // Россия и АТР.– 2014.– №4.– С.129–141

Кадочников П.А. О направлениях развития интеграционной повестки России и Китая // Рос. внешнеэкон. вестн.– 2015.– №1.– С.25–32

Канторович А.Э. Основные положения стратегии освоения природного газа Восточной Сибири и Дальнего Востока // Регион: экономика и социология. 2009. № 2. С. 96–109

Канторович А.Э., Коржубаев А.Г. Прогноз развития новых центров нефтяной и газовой промышленности на востоке России и экспорта нефти, нефтепродуктов и газа в восточном направлении // Регион: экономика и социология. 2007. № 1. С. 210–229

Капусткин В.И. Участие России в международных экономических организациях и соглашениях как фактор привлечения прямых зарубежных инвестиций / С.Ф. Сутырин, В.И. Капусткин // Актуальные проблемы экономического развития России. СПб.: Изд-во СПбГУ, 2002. - С. 229–250

Карпич В.А. Роль провинций во внешнеэкономическом развитии КНР и межрегиональные связи России и Китая / В.А. Карпич // Внешнеэкономический бюллетень. 2005. - № 5. - С. 31–35

Кашина Н.В. Инвестиционное сотрудничество Дальнего Востока РФ и Северо-Восточного Китая в добывающем секторе экономики // Проблемы Дал. Востока.– 2014.– №2.– С.100–108

Киселева В.В. Государственное регулирование инновационной сферы /В.В. Киселева, М.Г. Колосницына // ГУ ВШЭ, 2008. – 408 с. – С. 30

Котляров Н.Н. Зарубежный опыт формирования кластерных систем / Н.Н. Котляров, Л.В. Левченко // Экономические науки. 2014. № 119. – С. 105–110

Куприянов С.В. Особенности оценки региональных инновационных систем с учетом влияния кластерного развития / С.В. Куприянов, Е.А. Стрябкова, А.В. Заркович // Фундаментальные исследования. 2014. № 9-5. С. 1057–1061

Ледовский А.М. Стенограммы переговоров И.В. Сталина с Чжоу Эньлаем в августе-сентябре 1952 г. // Новая и новейшая история. 1997. № 2. С. 85–86

Ливенцев Н.Н. Внешняя торговля: взгляд в прошлое для движения в будущее / Н.Н. Ливенцев, Л.С. Ревенко // Вестник МГИМО Университета. 2011. – № 2. – С. 297–300

Ломакина Н.В. Промышленное развитие Дальнего Востока России и Северо-Востока Китая: цели, результаты и возможности для сотрудничества // ЭКО.– 2014.– №6.– С.25–39

Лузянин С.Г. Измерения российско-китайских отношений в АТЭС. Региональные факторы влияния и взаимодействий / С.Г. Лузянин // Китай в мировой и региональной политике. История и современность. 2012. – Т. 17. № 17. – С. 6–17

Лузянин С.Г. Экономический пояс шёлкового пути: модель 2015 года / С.Г. Лузянин, С.Л. Сазонов // Научно-аналитический журнал Обозреватель - Observer. 2015. – № 5 (304). С. – 35–46

Мастепанов А.М. Реализация «газового контракта» с Китаем: проблемы и возможности // Проблемы экономики и упр. нефтегазовым комплексом.– 2015.– №3.– С.4–11; №4.– С.4–10

Нехорошков В.П. Особенности межрегионального внешнеэкономического сотрудничества приграничных субъектов России и Китая / В.П. Нехорошков, А.В. Новикова // Научные проблемы транспорта Сибири и Дальнего Востока. 2014. № 4. – С. 18–21

Нечаев А. Дипломатия на экспорт. / Российская газета №12 8, от 3 июля 2003

Островский А.В. Россия и АТЭС: экономическая стратегия взаимодействия // Россия–Китай: развитие регионального сотрудничества в XXI веке: Второй междунар. форум, г. Маньчжурия– г. Чита, 2012 г.– Чита; Маньчжурия, 2012.– С.3–15

Пермякова Е.В. Современное состояние и перспективы российско-китайского экономического сотрудничества: автореферат диссертации на соискание ученой степени канд. экон. наук: 08.00.14 / Е. В. Пермякова. - М., 2009. - 25 с

Селищев А.С. Проблемы формирования модели инновационного экономического роста в России / А.С. Селищев, Т.А. Селищева // Вестник ИНЖЭКОНа. Серия: Экономика. 2013. – № 3 (62). – С. 9–16

Старкова Н.О. Обзор основных направлений российско-китайского сотрудничества / Н.О. Старкова, И.Г. Рзун, Е.В. Коновалова // Экономика и предпринимательство.– 2015.– №3 (56).– С.46–50

Стровский Л.Е. Состояние и проблемы модернизации промышленности Китая/ Л.Е. Стровский, Цзян Цзин // Экономика региона. 2011. – № 2. – С. 126–130

Сунь Яо. О путях повышения уровня китайско-российского сотрудничества // Проблемы Дал. Востока.– 2013.– №6.– С.88–92

Суходолов А.П. Байкальский регион как модельная территория устойчивого развития / А.П. Суходолов // Известия ИГЭА (электронная версия). – 2010. – №4

Суходолов А.П. Внешнеэкономические связи Иркутской области // Иркутская губерния. - Иркутск, №4(11), 2003

Суходолов А.П. Иркутская область: ресурсно-производственный потенциал // Ресурсы регионов России. – М., №3, 2004, с.32–43

Суходолов А.П. Пути совершенствования экономического сотрудничества Китая и России / А.П. Суходолов, Ван Нана // Изв. Иркут. гос. экон. акад.– 2013.– №6.– С.104–107

Суходолов Я.А. SWOT – анализ экономики современной России/ М.А. Балашова, Я.А. Суходолов // Исследование инновационного потенциала общества и формирование направлений его стратегического развития [текст]: материалы III международной научно-практической конференции (27 декабря 2013 года).– Курск: Юго-Западный государственный университет, 2013. – С.46–71

Суходолов Я.А. Повышение национальной конкурентоспособности России в контексте развития торгово-экономического сотрудничества с Китаем / И.В. Цвигун, М.А. Балашова, Я.А. Суходолов // Baikal Research Journal.– 2015. – Т.6, №5. – DOI:10.17150/2411-6262.2015.6(5).10

References

Суходолов Я.А. Анализ внешнеторговой деятельности России и регионов Сибирского федерального округа / Я.А. Суходолов // Приграничное сотрудничество и внешнеэкономическая деятельность: Исторический ракурс и современные оценки: Материалы Международной научной конференции 22–27 ноября 2012 г. (г. Чита Забайкальского края Российской Федерации – г. Эргуна Автономного района Внутренняя Монголия Китайской Народной Республики). – Чита: Изд-во Забайкал. гос. гум.-пед. ун-т. – Чита, 2012. – С. 270–275

Суходолов Я.А. Внешнеэкономическая деятельность Китая/ Я.А. Суходолов// Известия Иркутского государственного технического университета. – 2011. – №7 (54). – С. 158–161

Суходолов Я.А. Значение внешней торговли для экономического развития в современных условиях / Я.А. Суходолов // Седьмые востоковедные чтения БГУЭП: материалы международной научной конференции, посвященной 25-летнему юбилею кафедры мировой экономики и международного бизнеса. – Иркутск: Изд-во БГУЭП, 2013. – С. 157–165

Суходолов Я.А. Направления внешнеторгового сотрудничества Российской Федерации и Китайской Народной Республики / А.П. Суходолов, Я.А. Суходолов // Развитие сотрудничества приграничных регионов России и Китая: материалы международной научно-практической конференции, Маньчжурия, 24–25 сентября 2013 г. – Иркутск: Изд-во БГУЭП, 2014. – С. 31–47

Суходолов Я.А. Основные этапы развития торгово-экономических связей Иркутской губернии с Китайской Народной Республикой / Н. Ван, Я.А. Суходолов // Иркутский историко-экономический ежегодник: 2013. – Иркутск: Изд-во БГУЭП, 2013. – С. 184-190

Суходолов Я.А. Особенности статистического учета региональной внешнеторговой деятельности (на примере Иркутской области) / Я.А. Суходолов, И.В. Цвигун // Известия Иркутской государственной экономической академии. – 2012. – №1 (81). – С. 127–130

Суходолов Я.А. Повышение эффективности внешнеторговой деятельности как инструмент модернизации страны (на примере России и Китая)/ Я.А. Суходолов // Труды международной научно-практической конференции (2–5 июня 2011 г.) «Модернизация экономики и формирование технологических платформ» (ИНПРОМ– 2011). – Санкт-Петербург: Изд-во СПбПУ, 2011. – С. 552–560

Суходолов Я.А. Реализация восточной газовой программы и перспективы освоения газовых ресурсов Восточной Сибири / Я.А. Суходолов// Известия Иркутской государственной экономической академии. – 2014. – №6 (98). – С. 63–71

Суходолов Я.А. Роль внешнеэкономической деятельности в модернизации экономики России / Я.А. Суходолов// Известия Иркутской государственной экономической академии. – 2011. – №3 (77). – С. 115–118

Суходолов Я.А. Современное состояние внешней торговли Иркутской области / Я.А. Суходолов, И.В. Цвигун// Известия Иркутской государственной экономической академии (электронная версия). – 2013. [Электронный ресурс]. http://brj-bguep.ru/reader/article.aspx?id=17276

Суходолов Я.А. Современное состояние внешней торговли Сибирского Федерального округа / Я.А. Суходолов, И.В. Цвигун // Уровневое финансово-экономическое образование в России: проблемы внедрения компетентного подхода: в 2 ч. Ч.2: Материалы ежегодной международной научно-методической конференции и выездного заседания Учебно-методического совета УМО по специальности (профилю подготовки) «Мировая экономика». – М.: Финансовый университет, 2012. – С. 175–178

Суходолов Я.А. Современное состояние промышленного комплекса Иркутской области / Я.А. Суходолов // Экономика и управление (г. Санкт-Петербург). – 2014. – № 9 (107). – С. 75–78

Суходолов Я.А. Состояний и развитие инновационного потенциала в России и Китае / Я.А. Суходолов // Инновационный потенциал человека как ресурс социально-экономического развития региона: материалы межрегиональной научно-практической конференции, Чита 27–28 мая 2010 г.: ЧитГУ. – С. 83–89

Суходолов Я.А. Тенденции развития внешней торговли России/ Я.А.Суходолов // Интеграционные возможности современной экономики: материалы международной научно-практической конференции, г.Иркутск, 13–14 сентября 2012г. – Иркутск: Изд-во БГУЭП, 2012. – С.282–286

Суходолов Я.А. Тенденции развития внешнеэкономической деятельности КНР / Я.А. Суходолов И.В.Цвигун // Известия Иркутской государственной экономической академии. – 2010. – №2(70). – С.135–140

Суходолов Я.А. Этапы развития государственной системы регулирования внешней торговли России / Я.А.Суходолов // Историко-экономические исследования. – 2012. – Т.13, №1. – Иркутск: Изд-во БГУЭП, 2012. –С.129–143

Сюймин Сунь. Перспективы расширения российско-китайского экономического сотрудничества // Учен. зап. С.-Петерб. ун-та упр. и экономики. – 2014. – №1. – С.83–89

Титаренко М.Л. Концепция экономического пояса шелкового пути и интересы России / М.Л. Титаренко, А.Г. Ларин, В.А. Матвеев //Вестник Московского университета. Серия 25: Международные отношения и мировая политика. 2015. – Т. 7. № 1. – С. 3–43

Титаренко М.Л. Надежные российско-китайские отношения - основа развития и процветания наших стран / М.Л. Титаренко // Философские науки. 2015. – №1. – С. 7–11

Холодков В.Г. Можно ли использовать опыт Китая в модернизации России? // Россия и соврем. мир. – 2012. – №3(76). – С.97–107

Цуй Чжэн. Соразвитие и научно-техническое сотрудничество Дальнего Востока России и Северо-Восточного региона Китая // Гуманит., соц.- экон. и обществ. науки. – Краснодар, 2013. – №4. – С.319–324

Чжан Янчжи Влияние вступления России в ВТО на Китай Янчжи Чжан Журнал легко промышленного института Чжэн Чжоу. 2003, 3.С. 3–7

Чжао Хунту. Роль и место свободных экономических зон в развитии экономики Китая: Дис. канд. экон. наук: 08.00.14: М, 2000 185 с

Чжао Ч. Последствия вступления Китая в ВТО для экономики страны / Ч. Чжао // Известия ИГЭА. – 2006. – №4. – С. 107–109

Чистяков А.Н. Российско-китайские пограничные отношения на Дальнем Востоке: история и современность // Туризм: право и экономика. - М.: Юрист, 2009, № 1. - С. 11–14

Чу Лин. Сотрудничество между Китаем и Россией в газовой сфере в современных условиях // Россия и АТР. – 2015. – №1. – С.191–197

Шевченко И.В. Анализ структуры российско-китайского товарооборота в 2014г. / И. В.Шевченко, С.М.Симонян // Экономика устойчивого развития. 2014. № 4 (20). – С. 241–246

Ши Нинбо. Развитие отношений между Китаем и Советским Союзом в 80-е годы XX века: Дис. канд. ист. наук: 07.00.03, 07.00.15: Москва, 2003 167 с

2009 nian zhongguo qiye duiwaitouzi xiankuang baogao (Доклад о ситуации по инвестированию за рубеж китайскими предприятиями 2009 г.). [Электронный ресурс]. http://ccpit.org

Заявление первого посла делегации КНР при Всемирной торговой организации Сунь Чжэньой и действующего постоянного посла КНР при ВТО И.Сяочжунь о развитии китайской экономики после вступления КНР в ВТО 13.10.2011 [Электронный ресурс]. http://russian.cri.cn/881/2011/10/13/1s400319.htm

Интервью председателя КНР Ху Цзиньтао российским СМИ на кануне государственного визита в Россию и участия в церемонии открытия Года Китая в России 25.03.2007 [Электронный ресурс]. http://www.chineseembassy.org/rus/zxxx/t306867.htm

Исследование INSEAD: Глобальный индекс инноваций 2012 года. [Электронный ресурс] // Центр гуманитарных технологий. – 2012.07.06. http://gtmarket.ru/news/2012/07/06/4531

Исследование INSEAD: Глобальный индекс инноваций 2013 года. [Электронный ресурс] // Центр гуманитарных технологий. – 2013.07.01. http://gtmarket.ru/news/2013/07/01/6051

Официальный сайт «Газеты Коммерсантъ» [Электронный ресурс]. http://www.kommersant.ru/doc/1792299?themeid=198

References

Официальный сайт «Топ рейтинг» [Электронный ресурс]. http://top-rating.info/catalog/1/138/

Официальный сайт Высшей школы менеджмента Санкт-Петербургского государственного университета [Электронный ресурс]. http://www.gsom.spbu.ru/library/org

Официальный сайт Единого информационно-аналитического портала государственной поддержки инновационного развития бизнеса [Электронный ресурс]. http://innovation.gov.ru/taxonomy/term/545

Официальный сайт Института стратегического анализа и прогноза (ИСАП) [Электронный ресурс]. http://www.easttime.ru

Официальный сайт информационно-аналитического центра «Минерал» [Электронный ресурс]. http://www.mineral.ru/News/16392.html

Официальный сайт медиа компании «Deutsche Welle» [Электронный ресурс]. http://www.dw-world.de

Официальный сайт Международного общественного объединения «Развитие» [Электронный ресурс]. http://www.evolutio.info/content/view/988/168

Официальный сайт Министерства иностранных дер Российской Федерации [Электронный ресурс]. http://mid.ru/bdomp/ns-rasia.nsf/1083b7937ae580ae432569e7004199c2/c0ad76ab4c637e5643256c7900439b8e!OpenDocument

Официальный сайт Министерства финансов Российской Федерации [Электронный ресурс]. http://www.minfin.ru

Официальный сайт Народного банка Китая [Электронный ресурс]. http://www.pbc.gov.cn

Официальный сайт ОАО«Газпром» [Электронный ресурс]. http://www.gazprom.ru.

Официальный сайт Президента Российской Федерации [Электронный ресурс]. http://www.kremlin.ru/events/president/news/21063

Официальный сайт Территориального органа Федеральной службы государственной статистики по Иркутской области (Иркутскстат) [Электронный ресурс]. http://irkutskstat.gks.ru

Официальный сайт Торгового представительства Российской Федерации в Китайской народной республике [Электронный ресурс]. http://www.russchinatrade.ru/ru/ru-cn-cooperation/torg_ogran

Официальный сайт Федерального агентства по недропользованию Российской Федерации [Электронный ресурс]. http://www.rosnedra.gov.ru.

Официальный сайт Центра управления финансами [Электронный ресурс]. http://www.center-yf.ru/data/economy/Saldo-balansa.php

Рейтинг стран мира по уровню образования. Гуманитарная энциклопедия [Электронный ресурс] // Центр гуманитарных технологий. – 2009.10.10 (последняя редакция: 2015.03.18). http://gtmarket.ru/ratings/education-index/education-index-info

1996-2050 нянь Чжунго цзинцзи шэхуэй фачжань чжаньлюэ - цзоусян сяньдайхуады гоусян (1996-2050 гг.) [Стратегия социально-экономического развития Китая – на пути структурной модернизации]). Пекин, 1997. С. 468

Banken R. Die sowjetisch-chinesischen Beziehungen von 1949-1969 im Rahmen der weltweiten Interdependenz. Munster: LIT Verlag, 2005. – 190 с

Bauer W (1972, Spring) Import substitution and industrialization in Latin America: experiences and interpretations. Latin Am Res Rev 7(1):95–122

Yang L (2011) BRICS and the global transformation. Beijing

Carlsson B (2006) Internationalization of innovation systems: a survey of the literature. Res Policy 35(1):56–67

Charting China's Future (2011) Domestic and international challenges. In: Shambaugh D (ed) Routledge, London, New York, NY, p 187

Hugh D (2003) Good deeds and gundboats. Two centuries of American–Chinese encounters. Foreign Languages Press, Beijing, p 290

Elvidge CD, Baugh KE, Pack DW, Milesi C (2007) Satellite data estimate worldwide flared gas volumes. Oil Gas J 50–58

Sachs J (1985) External debt and macroeconomic performance in Latin America and East Asia. Brook Pap Econ Activity 2:523–573

Krugman P, Obstfeld M (2008) International economics: theory and policy. Prentice Hall, New York, NY, p 712

Mahtaney P (2007) India, China and globalization: the emerging superpowers and the future of economic development. Houndmills, p 256

Porter M (1998) Clusters and the new economics of competition. Harvard Bus Rev, p 220

Van C (2005) The future of the petrochemical industry in Europe. Catal Today 106:15–29

Whalley J, Xin X (2010) China's FDI and non-FDI economies and the sustainability of future high Chinese growth. China Econ Rev 21:123–135

Lin Y, Cai F, Li Z (1996) Cato J 16(2):201–231

Го Теминь. Чжунго цзинцзи дэ фачжань юй гайгэ: [Развитие и реформа китайской экономики: в 2 т.]. Пекин, 2011

Е Юнле. Дэн Сяопин тайбянь чжунго 1978: чжунго минъюнь да чжуаньчжэ (Дэн Сяопин изменил Китай. 1978: судьбоносный поворот в истории Китая). Наньчан: Цзянси жэньминь чубаньшэ, 2008. - 462 с

Майсян цюаньмянь сяокан: синьдэ 10 нянь: [10 лет по пути к полному построению общества сяокан] / ред. Чжан Юйтай. Пекин, 2010

Оуя Цзинцзи, №1, 2015. Экономика России, Восточной Европы и Центральной Азии. Пекин, Институт России, Восточной Европы и Центральной Азии, 2014. – 128 с

Суходолов Я.А. Развитие торгово-экономических связей Иркутской области с Китаем / Н. Ван, Я.А.Суходолов // Журнал Тяньцзиньского колледжа менеджмента. – Тяньцзинь, 2014.– №3. – С.34–35

Чжунгодэ фачжань: шицзедэ тяочжань хайши цзиюй (Развитие Китая: вызов или шанс для мира). Ред. Чжоу Чжицинь. Пекин: Дандай шицзе, 2006. – 131 с

Элосы хуанпишу. Элосы фачжань баогао 2014. Желтая книга по России. Ежегодный отчет по развитию в России. 2014 г. Ред. Ли Юнцюань. Пекин, Шэхуй кэсюэ вэньсянь чубаньшэ, 2014. – 289 с